PSYCHOLOGY IN FOOTBALL

C000217457

- How can the skills of the sport psychologist be put to best use within a football club?
- How can a sport psychologist help elite footballers perform at their maximum level?

In this groundbreaking guide to the role of the sport psychologist within elite and professional football, leading sport psychologist Mark Nesti argues that working closely with coaches and players to create a receptive environment is vital if psychologists are to add maximum value to team and individual performances.

Drawing on a decade's professional experience working at the top level of English football, Nesti offers a detailed guide to delivering sport psychology in an elite team sport environment, from practical drills on the training field to shaping organizational behaviour at club level. The book explores the full range of issues and themes that define the role of the professional sport psychologist working in football today, including:

- Mental skills training
- Group cohesion and team dynamics
- Counselling, trust and confidentiality
- Transitions in football
- Managerial and coaching philosophies
- Structure, communication and organizational psychology

The book is illustrated throughout with real-world case studies, drawing on research into sixteen professional clubs across five European countries, and concludes by suggesting how other elite team sports can learn from the experiences of professional football. This is the only book to outline a holistic approach to psychology in football and the only book to offer such a rich combination of theory and practice. It is therefore essential reading for all students of sport psychology and all psychologists and coaches working in elite team sport.

Mark Nesti is Reader in Sport Psychology at Liverpool John Moores University. He has worked as a consultant sport psychologist with four English Premier League football clubs, and is currently working with players and staff at three Premiership clubs.

PSYCHOLOGY IN FOOTBALL

WORKING WITH ELITE AND PROFESSIONAL PLAYERS

MARK NESTI

Routledge
Taylor & Francis Group

LONDON AND NEW YORK

First published 2010
by Routledge
2 Park Square, Milton Park, Abingdon, Oxon, OX14 4RN

Simultaneously published in the USA and Canada
by Routledge
711 Third Avenue, New York, NY 10017

*Routledge is an imprint of the Taylor & Francis Group,
an informa business*

© 2010 Mark Nesti

Typeset in Melior
by Pindar NZ, Auckland, New Zealand
Printed and bound in Great Britain
by TJ International Ltd, Padstow, Cornwall

All rights reserved. No part of this book may be reprinted
or reproduced or utilised in any form or by any electronic,
mechanical, or other means, now known or hereafter
invented, including photocopying and recording, or in any
information storage or retrieval system, without permission
in writing from the publishers.

British Library Cataloguing in Publication Data
A catalogue record for this book is available from the British
Library

Library of Congress Cataloging in Publication Data
Nesti, Mark, 1959–
Psychology in football: working with elite and professional
players / by Mark Nesti.
     p. cm.
  Includes bibliographical references and index.
  1. Football—Psychological aspects. I. Title.
  GV959.N37 2010
  796.33201—dc22   2010007487

ISBN13: 978-0-415-54999-8 (pbk)
ISBN13: 978-0-415-54998-1 (hbk)
ISBN13: 978-0-203-87458-5 (ebk)

For Sarah

CONTENTS

FOREWORD

Sport psychology has not always been well received in the world of professional football. This might appear to be a surprising statement to make about one of the most high profile, intense and pressured sports on the global stage. Especially at Premier League levels the rewards for success and punishment for failure are arguably unlike anything else in our culture, with the possible exception of high level politics. Although at the highest levels of the game there is a far greater knowledge about the importance of the mental side to performing well, those wishing to offer a sports psychology service in professional football often face a considerable number of obstacles. Misunderstandings, unrealistic expectations, suspicions and doubt can be found on both sides. Many sport psychologists are reluctant to work in the sport, and there are those in the game who question the value of employing sport psychologists.

Mark Nesti is someone whose experience in this sport at the highest level makes him an ideal person to write about what it is like to deliver sport psychology in professional football. I met him almost ten years ago at a sport psychology conference on working with teams. If I remember correctly, his message was similar to much of what is in this book- psychological work with individuals is most effective when the sport psychologist engages with and understands the culture of the sport, club and the team. I thought that this hit the spot for me as a young and new sport psychologist in a Premiership club, where I was quickly finding out that mental skills training would be a very small part of my job, and that dealing with broader issues and managing the environment would be the key task.

This book is essentially about some of the reasons for this state of affairs. Although aimed at sport psychologists, students and those wishing to work in this field, this is not a one sided account which simplistically blames clubs for their failure to embrace the discipline. But neither does this book have little to say to the clubs themselves. A major strength of what has been written is that Mark Nesti has attempted to get behind the difficulties facing psychologists and clubs in this area of work, and has identified a way forward that is both realistic and achievable. That he has been able to do this owes much to the extensive involvement that Mark has had delivering sport psychology support within a number of Premiership clubs and with professional football staff and players during the last 15 years.

Much of the written material that currently exists on sport psychology can be divided into self help type literature, or academic publications in research journals. Although both of these can be useful on occasion, the former often lacks depth and sounds like common sense, whilst the latter rarely seems to consider the broader culture within which the action should take place. An impressive feature of this text is that it includes reference to complex concepts and psychological theory that will challenge the reader, but provide a sometimes new and often richer account than exists in many other books addressing sport psychology. Equally important, consideration is given to the topics of environment and culture. Having worked in Premier League football for a decade I have discovered that developing and managing the culture, streamlining organisational processes and systems, and affecting policies and operational practices are crucial areas for the sport psychologist to influence. Although these tasks are often carried out by performance directors in some clubs, there is a role here for sport psychologists to take beyond the individual work on performance enhancement carried out with players and staff.

I hope that this book will help sport psychologists to prepare themselves to face up to the reality of delivering sport psychology in the wonderfully exciting but incredibly challenging world of professional football. For some, this may mean that they will have to learn new skills or even engage with unfamiliar ideas and theory. Clubs and the sport itself can also benefit from having a better understanding of what the sport psychologist can bring to the party - something that ultimately will be able to enhance the performance of both staff and players.

Mike Forde
Director of Football Operations,
Chelsea FC,
May, 2010

ACKNOWLEDGEMENTS

This task felt at times like a challenge too far. Life seems to be getting so frantic for many of us in our unhealthy postmodern world that it is increasingly difficult to find periods of quiet and stillness to be able to think deeply about things, and maybe even write about them on occasion. The most important person who has helped me find the necessary time in the midst of all this bustle has been my wife, Sarah. Without her sacrifices and unswerving support this work would never have come to fruition.

In my professional role at Liverpool John Moores University I have been greatly helped by many colleagues, especially Drs Martin Eubank, Martin Littlewood and Dave Richardson, who have covered my tasks when I have been overrun, and whose knowledge about psychology, football and culture has contributed to ideas expressed in this book. Professor Tim Cable, Head of the School of Sport and Exercise Sciences at LJMU, has been remarkably supportive in facilitating my involvement in Premiership football. This is no easy or simple thing to do, particularly when universities, like other sectors, are operating in a difficult financial and economic climate.

I would also like to acknowledge the part played by Mike Forde, Director of Football Operations at Chelsea FC, Sam Allardyce, Manager of Blackburn Rovers, and Mark Taylor, Head of Sports Medicine and Sports Science at Fulham FC, in my development and understanding of the role that sport psychology can play in Premiership football. Many other individuals in the game during the past fifteen years have taught me much about performance, professional football culture and psychology; but these three people have made the biggest contribution to my knowledge and skills.

Lastly, I must convey my gratitude for the extremely patient help that I have received from Simon Whitmore and Joshua Wells at Routledge. I know the deadline extensions were a great help to me, but that it put you under increasing pressure. Without such flexibility I am sure this work would have been impossible to complete.

INTRODUCTION

Increasing numbers of sport psychologists have been working in professional sport since the early 2000s. The particular demands and challenges faced by sport psychologists operating in team sport environments is something that has arguably not been adequately considered within the literature. Professional team sports cultures, such as those found in football, are entirely different from what is usually encountered in lower-level and amateur sporting environments.

Delivering sport psychology so as to be effective and welcomed is something the sport psychologist has always to face. Whilst there are many reasons for this, one may be closely related to the type of academic literature that has prevailed in the discipline thus far. It has been pointed out on numerous occasions that there is a lack of theoretical breadth in much of the research literature within sport psychology, and that mental skills training seems to have dominated approaches to applied practice until very recently. This situation has probably contributed to the problems encountered by sport psychologists working in professional sports like football. Mental skills such as imagery, self-talk, relaxation techniques and goal-setting are rarely sufficient. The scope of issues and environmental demands facing the sport psychologist working in professional football means that something else is required. Many successful practitioners faced with this dilemma have attempted to survive by pursuing other qualifications to complement their sport psychology knowledge, or have relied on previous experience and common sense to guide their approach. Although this is understandable, it does nothing to support arguments about the professionalization of sport psychology.

This book is aimed at upper-level undergraduate and postgraduate students, and at sport psychologists who wish to work within professional football. It is also written for those many applied sport psychologists who are deeply dissatisfied with the discipline's over-reliance on mental skills training and research that often seems to ask more and more, about less and less. Since football is the most successful and wealthiest sport in the world, it would be surprising if greater opportunities for sport psychologists to work in the game did not continue to expand. However, there are already a significant number of sport psychologists working in professional football, usually in a part-time capacity, and most often at youth and academy levels. These individuals and others working in first-team settings frequently criticize the education and the training they received to help them succeed in their role. Many of these predominately young people and inexperienced psychologists are strongly critical of the continued dominance of the positivist research they encountered within their educational experiences. There is also negative comment about how inappropriate and ineffective psychological skills training can be especially at first team levels and with young professionals.

These courageous newly qualified sport psychologists and consultants are managing to maintain a critical perspective towards their role and the discipline of sport psychology. They usually acquired this skill and developed it throughout their earlier formal educational experiences, especially at university. Unfortunately, this approach is not always apparent within the university sector, where the US mantra of 'publish or perish' seems to be taking hold on this side of the Atlantic as well. This has been one of several key factors in narrowing the theoretical base and range of research topics evident within the academic journals within sport and exercise psychology. Ideally, this literature should provide a constant source of useful material for those working in the field to assimilate and translate into practice. It is argued here that this is not happening and, in fact, the situation may actually be worse now than two or more decades ago when there was a smaller community within sport psychology itself.

In some ways, it could be claimed that we have two distinct cultures. One is interested in pursuing research in to an ever decreasing number of topics, whilst the other ignores the findings from such work, and frequently operates in an atheoretical and practical way. If this situation occurred in medicine, education or other established professional areas

2

within the caring professions, there would be great concern. A quick glance at the contents page in many of our most important sport psychology journals suggests that we are still for the most part engaged in examining the efficacy of various mental skills techniques, and investigating factors associated with stress, competitive anxiety and motivation. That almost all of this work is derived from behavioural, cognitive and cognitive-behavioural approaches in psychology, or continues to rely on using self-report instruments to collect data, appears to be of little concern to some of those charged with helping the area to grow and become more ecologically valid.

There is little mention of mental skills training within this book. This is deliberate. The material used throughout is based on the author's experience of almost a decade of delivering sport psychology support within Premiership clubs and with professional footballers. Many of the ideas, concepts and information mentioned in the book have been gathered from several other sport psychologists who have previously been active within the game, or who still work in Premiership and elite professional football. This book, therefore, is primarily about practice. However, as would be expected in any description of professional practice, there are accounts of theory and relevant research to support descriptions and recommendations. This is not meant to be a comprehensive summary of all sport psychology research in football. Rather, the aim has been to address the task from the opposite angle. Following the requirements of phenomenology, data based on the experiences of those who are closest to the action, namely the players and their support staff and coaches, has provided the empirical evidence for this account. This has meant that new concepts such as existential anxiety, identity, values and spirit have been included, especially where they can help to explain the day-to-day experiences of the sport psychologist operating in elite professional football.

The psychological perspective that has been used most fully in this work is opposed to materialist, reductionist and natural science accounts of psychology. The work presented here is closest to humanistic and certain existential psychology approaches, and is based on a conceptualization of psychology as a human science (Giorgi 1970). This means that focus is on the person first and the athlete second. This, after all, is what Martens (1987) demanded of sport psychology over thirty years

3

ago. This point has also been supported by Corlett (1996a) and Ravizza (2002a). It is notable that the work of these three individuals focuses on the concept of person rather than the notion of individuals.

A person is considered to be mind, body and spirit and, as such, this and only this can claim to be a fully holistic perspective. Such a view of course demands that psychology does not restrict itself to the study of the isolated individual, but, instead, is prepared to examine people in their broader environment and culture. Because of this, existential psychology will be used to inform much of the work contained in this book. This is because of three main reasons. First, existential psychology is the approach most associated with phenomenology. Phenomenology demands that all research and applied work must start with the 'lived experiences' of the clients or subjects. In this way, phenomenology claims to be a strictly empirical approach. The second reason is that the roots of existentialism are European rather than North American. This includes the destructive self-centred and nihilistic relativism associated with Sartre (1958) and the more hopeful, optimistic and spiritual brand of Marcel (1948) and others. The important factor though as far as sport psychology is concerned is that it was historically the precursor to the humanistic psychology approach that is associated most usually with Maslow (1968). However, unlike humanistic psychology and so-called positive psychology, the existential view recognizes that both positive and negative events and experiences can ultimately benefit the growth and development of persons in sport and life in general. This perspective seems particularly well suited to the environment of elite professional football where players repeatedly experience incredibly positive and exciting moments alongside periods of great difficulty, that require sacrifice, responsibility and the making of difficult choices. Finally, existential psychology, in common with the psychoanalytic psychology espoused by psychology's first and arguably most important theorist, Sigmund Freud (1991) claims that anxiety is *the* most important psychological factor. Existential ideas are not merely restricted to competitive anxiety, but extend to consider anxiety in much broader terms. Again, it is important to note that this approach views normal anxiety as a potentially positive experience (Nesti 2007). Premiership football is riddled with the experience of anxiety. Similar to the ideas expressed by Corlett (1996a), this approach suggests that anxiety should

4

more often be confronted and used constructively to aid choices and accepting responsibility, rather than being managed away through mental skills techniques.

In conclusion, the theory, concepts and research that underpins the material contained in this book has been selected to help deepen understanding about the experiences of delivering sport psychology in elite and Premiership football. Issues like being dropped from the starting 11 despite being a mentally focused, appropriately motivated and highly experienced player are often not matters that can be dealt with through mental skills training or psychological techniques. Similarly, player–coach relationships, dealing with the demands of new cultures, seeking to move clubs, or attempting to deal with the threats of relegation and or of being sold, are some of the real issues faced by players over a typical season. Sport psychologists need psychological approaches and theory that will be 'up to the task' of dealing with such matters.

The book is ordered in such a way that the first chapters attempt to address some of the daily, weekly or season-long practical issues that the sport psychologist may have to deal with in a Premiership club or in elite professional football. The second part of the book focuses more on some of the broader considerations and conceptual issues that are always in the background when engaged in this type of work. For example, topics like values, confidentiality and the importance of the identity of the sport psychologist, the team, and the coaching staff is included. Much of this has received little recognition to date in the sport psychology literature dealing with elite professional sport.

Chapter 1 examines the unique culture of Premiership football and elite professional clubs. It is absolutely essential that the sport psychologist gains an understanding of this environment as quickly as possible. It is also vital to avoid the many and varied pitfalls existing in this culture, to develop a way of fitting into the environment and become a skilled reader of the conventions, traditions and practices in this type of world. This as a highly volatile, performance-focused and pressured environment, which places special demands on everyone who works in this milieu. Sport psychologists and their effectiveness will be under close scrutiny in this type of single-minded culture from day one.

Chapter 2 addresses more familiar territory for some sport psychologists.

Counselling is increasingly being used in sport psychology practice to ensure that athletes are able to discuss things that are most important to them, rather than learning to use psychological techniques that may fail to meet their needs. This chapter asks how an existential psychology counselling approach can provide a theoretical underpinning to one-to-one work with Premiership players and elite professional footballers.

Chapter 3 continues in a similar vein. Focus is on how the sport psychologist can support the coaching team and help with staff development. This role seems close to that of an organizational psychologist, and can involve writing staff job descriptions, facilitating development away days, and supporting continuing professional development for staff. Following on from this account, Chapter 4 deals with the type of one-to-one support that the sport psychologist can provide for the manager. Some of this task can also be effectively carried out by sport psychologists based at the club, part or full time, or through support from external consultants outside the football club. Where the sport psychologist has a great deal of contact with the manager and is immersed in the club, he or she may be able to work closely and confidentially with the manager to assist them in their role and future development.

Team-building, team cohesion and team spirit are considered essential at all levels of sport. Chapter 5 discusses what these terms mean by drawing on little-used concepts and theoretical accounts. Some of these are located within the parent discipline of psychology and may provide a new impetus to understanding and application within sport psychology. Chapter 6 continues with the theme of support by focusing on the role of the liaison officer. This individual, in many ways like the club chaplain, is often highly skilled at providing pastoral support where the focus is not explicitly on performance and the competitive process. This chapter considers how the liaison officer and sport psychologist can collaborate to best effect. The penultimate chapter investigates important ideas about confidentiality, trust and values. Within an elite professional sport environment, these terms will help the sport psychologist to guide their work in a professional and effective way. Chapter 7 also includes reference to team and individual identity. Existential and humanistic psychology perspectives have emphasized that identity and personal meaning are crucial elements in understanding how people, or groups, deal with success and failure. Although many in psychology

6

and sport psychology may be surprised to see reference to values in a book about professional sport, those who adopt a human science approach recognize that psychology's roots in philosophy mean that this is a legitimate and important topic.

The final chapter concludes with a consideration of how the experiences of delivering sport psychology in elite professional football relates to other professional team sport environments. There are very few empirical articles within the scientific journals, with the exception of Rotella (1990) that deal in detail with professional sport. It is hoped that, in the future, those working in other professional team sport environments will write accounts of the particular demands, requirements and challenges facing sport psychologists in these other arenas of applied practice.

The material presented here owes much to the support I received from managers, assistant managers, first-team coaches, performance directors, sports scientists and other support staff at Bolton Wanderers, Newcastle United and Hull City during nine seasons (2001–2009) in Premiership football. During this period my part-time engagement amounted to an average of three or four days a week involvement at each club. This level of contact allowed me the opportunity to live the role from the inside, whilst always being somewhat independent from the club and the organization. This book is also based on my work as a sport psychologist with mostly first-team players and young professionals from these clubs, and from others I have supported in professional football since 1995. The vignettes and anonymized accounts contained in some chapters of the book draw on the experiences with players and staff throughout this period; however, to protect all these individuals, none of these accounts is meant to represent real cases, but are more usually an amalgamation of issues and experiences encountered delivering sport psychology in elite professional football.

1

KNOWING PROFESSIONAL FOOTBALL

UNDERSTANDING THE CULTURE

This chapter looks at the importance of understanding the particular, even unique, culture that exists within a professional football club, especially in the Premiership. Culture refers to much more than explicit processes, operational mechanisms and daily practices. It includes all these factors and others that are harder to identify clearly but which nevertheless have a significant impact on the working environment. Factors here include tradition, unwritten rules, precedents, values and patterns of belief. If some of these terms sound somewhat philosophical it should not surprise us. An organization's culture is determined more by the ideals that govern it, the vision it pursues and values it adheres to. These ideas in turn are grounded in philosophy, whether overtly acknowledged or not.

Several authors (e.g. Relvas *et al.* 2010) have recently claimed that sport psychologists will be largely ineffective in delivering their work in sports organizations where they fail to understand the culture they are operating within. Empirical research (Woodman and Hardy 2001) has identified a number of important organizational stressors that sport performers, coaches and others must cope with in order to achieve their aims. These include communication failures, role conflict and role ambiguity, and a lack of clarity about role overload. The challenges that face sport psychologists operating in Premiership football clubs or other elite sport organizations are no different. They must provide their service within an environment where there are other distracting influences, such as media interest, the activities of agents and contract negotiations.

Other sources of organizational stress may include rapid changes in playing and coaching personnel, interdepartmental infighting, interference from club owners in team affairs and unrealistic demands on family life. This research has arguably helped alert sport psychologists to many of the important obstacles and challenges that they will face in a club or team. The main aim of this chapter is to show that this does not complete the picture. Without a full understanding of the cultural milieu existing within an organization little can be achieved, and the sport psychologist in professional sport is likely to feel frustrated and unappreciated and may even be largely ignored. Within a fast-paced, ruthless and 'win at all costs' environment, sport psychologists who fail to read the cultural matrix may well have their contracts terminated, that is, unless they resign beforehand.

This chapter draws on the experiences I have had on the inside of three Premiership clubs over nine seasons and is also based on years of individual work with professional footballers and coaching staff from a range of clubs. This work cannot be described as research since it has typically involved consultancy projects lasting between six years and two–three months. As such, these reflections on the importance of culture in professional football, and Premiership football more specifically, emerged from engaging in traditional performance-enhancement focused psychological work. As an applied practitioner, my understanding about the importance of culture to my work as a sport psychologist has grown and evolved over time. Already possessing a good degree of knowledge about professional football prior to working with the sport, I had always expected that knowing the game and its ways of working from the inside would be important. What I did not fully appreciate was that being able to analyse this culture and operate alongside its idiosyncratic qualities would be vital to my capability of working in this sport at the highest level.

This chapter is not intended to provide a list of definitions and conceptual accounts surrounding the term culture. Instead, it will attempt to describe some of the most pertinent factors within the culture of a Premiership football club that will be most likely to affect the work of sport psychologists and their successs in their role. Part of this approach will be devoted to suggesting how the psychologist can influence cultural change and offer ideas that can be used by those charged with impacting on this in performance sport environments. Each section will attempt to examine what type of knowledge and personal qualities the psychologist will need to work effectively within a professional football club, especially in the Premiership.

Recommendations will also be offered in relation to changes that need to take place to better prepare students and recently qualified sport psychologists who may wish to work in this area.

SETTING THE SCENE

The Premier League is quite easily the biggest game in town. Whether the criteria are financial, media interest, global reach or levels of passion, the Premier League dominates the British sporting scene. Recent figures reveal that English Premier League broadcasting rights have increased over the 1997–2007 period from 49 million GBP to 568 million GBP revenue (The Political Economy of Football 2008). Although many commentators within the world of sport and beyond have criticized this unhealthy dominance, the fact remains that, for the time being, Premier League clubs exist in the most successful professional sports league outside the United States. Given this level of wealth and the huge and diverse interest in Premier League football, one would expect an equivalent professional culture to exist in the clubs. Although every club will differ in relation to how close it comes to matching a fully professional ethos, there are common features that are found in most clubs. The most beneficial of these relate to the huge resources that clubs have in terms of highly qualified staff, state-of-the-art stadiums, modern training complexes and sophisticated commercial, marketing and sponsorship arms. As Brady *et al.* have pointed out, 'professional football represents a near-perfect market for human talent', and especially at Premiership levels it, 'provides a model of management where only best practice succeeds' (2008: 58–60).

However, this particularly positive view of the Premiership and professional football is not always apparent to those working at the sharp end. It is now time to turn our attention to where clubs fail to operate in accordance with authentic professional values. These professional failings exist for a number of reasons. Some of these are due to external conditions imposed upon the game and the clubs in particular. Others are more the result of tradition, ethical codes and internal pressures. Taken together these factors constitute the culture of the club. Sport psychologists need to fully understand the negative and unprofessional aspects of this culture if they wish to be able to carry out their job properly and deliver their services effectively.

In my experience the most important relationship for sport psychologists is that between themselves and the manager. Although the psychologist may consider that their most important role is to support the players to enhance their performance, little can be achieved without the active and visible support of the manager. Credibility with the playing staff can be lost or gained in an instant depending on the way a manager relates to the sport psychologist. The reasons behind this are complex and have been little discussed within the sport psychology literature. This is not about whether the manager 'gets on with' the sport psychologist and likes them on a personal level. The cultural problem is much more deep-rooted and profound than this.

PREVIOUS ENCOUNTERS WITH SPORT PSYCHOLOGISTS

A manager's understanding of the value of sport psychology often reflects his previous experiences with psychologists. Although within a British context sport psychologists are often accredited through the British Association of Sport and Exercise Sciences (BASES) or the British Psychological Society (BPS), many do not posses these, or any other recognized qualifications. Whilst there are arguably some competent practitioners without qualifications in sport psychology and psychology, there are many others who lack the necessary skills and knowledge to work effectively and ethically. This is compounded by the fact that many calling themselves psychologists are keen to work in this lucrative, high-profile and exciting sector. In my experience, professional football at the highest levels seems to attract offers of work from a highly diverse range of individuals who sometimes make remarkable claims about their competencies and effectiveness.

Contact from various assorted guru-type individuals is unfortunately common. They include those who promise to convert the team mindset

12

to one where defeat will never be encountered again, to those claiming that they can change the aura surrounding particular players through telepathic techniques delivered from 4,000 miles away. There are also less extreme examples, especially from individuals and consultancies with experience of working in the corporate business sector. Some of these individuals are exceptionally capable and can help clubs, staff and players in areas like goal-setting, motivation and leadership training and development. I have worked closely with consultants who have this set of skills and contextual knowledge, and they have sometimes proved to be helpful in shaping cultural practices and strategy in particular. Managers, coaches and other sport science and medical staff can have a positive view of the support provided by such individuals and organizations, seeing as a strength their ability to operate in fast-moving and volatile business environments.

These two different types of psychology services have impacted considerably on the perceptions that managers and other key staff hold about what sport psychologists should be able to do for a club and the team. For example, on occasion, sport psychologists in Premiership football are viewed positively because they are seen as experts in organizational psychology (in the same way as business or occupational psychologists). However, Nesti and Littlewood (2009) have argued that this frequently presents most qualified sport psychologists with a problem because their education and training has inadequately prepared them for this role. From a more negative point of view, staff and players at the club may dismiss the value of sport psychologists because of their previous encounters with the many cranks and charlatans attracted to this sport. I myself have had to face this in many ways. For example, I have had been variously referred to as the 'wizard', 'spirit', or 'psycho' over the nine seasons I worked inside various Premier League clubs, a fact that captures at a prosaic level this underlying misunderstanding and mistrust about sport psychologists. Sometimes players and staff show a degree of disrespect for the sport psychologist. Refusal to use the psychologist's professional title where this is appropriate, referring to them by their surname or using derogatory terms to describe their role are just some of the unprofessional and unethical behaviours that are commonplace in this environment. Parker's (1995) ethnographic research in professional football describes these types of experience as being in keeping with those found in many working-class masculine environments where sensitivity to the feelings and perceptions of others is frowned upon.

EVIDENCE OF WORTH

Another potential obstacle to being fully accepted and valued in this culture is that the manager, chairman and other influential figures at the club may demand evidence of tangible outcomes from the activities of the sport psychologist. This may appear to be a reasonable expectation; however, recent literature in the field of applied sport psychology has identified that this is not a simple or easy requirement to satisfactorily address. Anderson *et al.* (2004) have discussed the difficulties facing the sport psychologist in providing evidence about their effectiveness, challenges related to the evaluation of their effectiveness and the value of quantitative data in this context. One of the problems that the sport psychologist will immediately encounter in Premiership clubs is that most clubs now utilize performance analysis data (e.g. Prozone) that captures physical and technical outputs from matches and training. Alongside extensive medical records on injuries, nutrition and anthropometrical data, the manager and club staff are increasingly used to dealing with vast amounts of quantifiable information, and statistics on individual players and opposing teams.

Sport psychologists are in some ways faced with a dilemma that extends beyond issues around measurement and evaluation. Psychology as an academic discipline is riven with disputes about the value of so-called hard data against more subjective soft data. This debate is rooted in the older dispute about whether psychology is a natural science able to identify cause and affect relationships, or whether it is a human science discipline which can only legitimately report on relationships between data. In the highly charged and demanding culture of Premier League football, there is an understandable desire for objective information and rigorous data that can be used by the manager and senior staff to guide their decisions.

At times, the sport psychologist may feel pressured to provide hard data about players' mental skills, motivational orientations or their anxiety levels, in order to meet the expectations of the coaches and manager.

14

However, Giorgi (2000) has argued that, since psychology is a human science, its main function is to focus on the perceptions and subjective meaning that individuals attach to events and to record or report this data as clearly and completely as possible. This view has been supported by Ravizza (2002a) and Nesti (2004) in sport psychology. They argue that it is impossible to get objective data in psychology because of free will. That is, no experience or event will be interpreted exactly the same way by any two people because human beings are unique in that they are not just products of their environment or their genes, but have the capacity to think freely. This has been referred to by existential phenomenological psychology as situated freedom (Nesti 2004).

The task facing the sport psychologist in this situation involves a process of education about what sport psychology data can reasonably be expected to provide. In my experience sport psychologists can do immense damage by promising that their data can provide something on a par with natural sciences such as physiology or biomechanics. Managers and other key staff may push for this level of certainty, especially at times when they are facing important moments and difficult choices.

However, sport psychologists should be careful because it is not uncommon for this approach to result in their own effectiveness being assessed through changes in objective data. They must think carefully beforehand about the type of evaluation they would feel is most empirical (i.e. real). If they claim that psychological data is no different from that provided by the other natural sciences, they need to be ready to retain their job at the club based on an assessment of this and nothing else.

ARE YOU WORTH IT?

As with all organizations, pressure on resources means that decisions are made about what services are offered to players and which staff are employed. The decision to take on a sport psychologist in a full-time or part-time role will also be influenced by the demand for other types of support. The manager and chairman may be convinced that a sport psychologist would be of benefit to the team; however, budget constraints often make this a harder choice than it may at first appear. Can they justify taking on a sport psychologist instead of another physiotherapist, or member of the coaching team? What about someone else to assist with the performance analysis of players in reserve team matches, or a nutritionist to help with ensuring that optimum dietary needs are met for each player and that these are evaluated scientifically? Given such tough choices, and without a thorough understanding of what a sport psychologist can bring to the club, managers and their chairman may feel reluctant to bring a sport psychologist into this environment.

Even where a sport psychologist is employed there are a number of other potential problems that are often encountered in this culture. Many of the interactions between the sport psychologist and individual players or members of staff are often carried out in a low key, informal and *ad hoc* fashion. Andersen (2000) has referred to this as 'hanging out', something that takes place across a number of sports where formal access to players may often be difficult to organize. There are occasions when this approach can represent a powerful way to engage in psychological work with staff or players within such a volatile and time-pressured environment. A major drawback of this approach concerns the issues of evaluation and visibility. This way of working, similar to more formal pre-planned one-to-one meetings, requires some level of privacy, and might even sometimes take place away from the club's training venue. This means that unlike, say, the work of coaches or physical therapists, much of what the sport psychologist does is often unseen and unnoticed. Although records of more formal meetings that the sport psychologist may keep at the club at least offer evidence that some work is taking place there, this still lacks the immediate physical visibility so apparent in other activities at the club.

BEING ONE OF THE GUYS!

Richardson *et al.* (2004) have argued that the climate within most professional football clubs, in the UK at least, is an aggressively masculine one, whereby players are socialized into hiding their true feelings and encouraged to display 'macho' behaviours. Psychology is sometimes viewed in this type of culture as feminine and weak. It may be denigrated for concerning itself with feelings, emotions and understanding,

16

all of which are castigated for being associated with stereotypically feminine ways of thinking and acting.

Sport psychologists who are prepared to throw themselves into the physical activities that may be a part of pre-season training exercises, or team-building events, have a great advantage over those who adopt a more withdrawn role. The opportunity to share in masculine camaraderie and join in the ubiquitous 'banter' that is so much a part of this culture will do much to mitigate the feminine stereotype. If the psychologist has also been a former athlete, or, even better, played football to a good standard, there will be a greater acceptance of their role and function. This clearly means that female sport psychologists will face a different set of challenges, especially if they have not played the game. Interestingly, there are some female practitioners working in professional football who are well accepted, especially where they deliver psychology within their remit as education and welfare officers and with youth players. A possible advantage for a female sport psychologist in professional football culture is that at least she will not be viewed negatively – because she is delivering a service that is traditionally seen as rather feminine.

WE ARE THE SPORT PSYCHOLOGISTS!

As has been reported by researchers such as Brown and Potrac (2009), it is quite common to find that elite-level coaches tend to view themselves as unofficial sport psychologists. This is understandable given that, as has been acknowledged elsewhere (e.g. Williams 2006), the higher the level of sport performer the more important are their mental skills and psychological qualities. For example, Crust (2007) has claimed that most research into mental toughness reveals that superior athletes are more mentally tough than those at a lower level. To be effective and successful, coaches and managers in Premier League and professional football must be skilled communicators and be able to deal with increasingly diverse groups of individuals in their teams. Much of their work on and off the training ground involves providing feedback to players as a group or on an individual basis, and giving inspirational and motivational talks pre-match and at half-time. Those managers and senior coaches whom I have been able to observe closely on the training ground and in the home and away changing rooms at some of the biggest clubs in world football are often excellent communicators, with the capacity to read the mood of a group and to target their comments towards the individual player where necessary. Many of these skills and competencies have been acquired 'on the job', and are the result of years of careful observation and patient reflection. Sport psychologists will have to add something to the knowledge and methods adopted by managers and coaches if they are to gain credibility and justify their professional qualifications and academic credentials. The frequently encountered belief that managers and senior coaches have little to learn from professional sport psychologists reflects a deep suspicion of academic learning, which is seen as opposed to acquiring knowledge and understanding through practice and experience. British professional football, including the Premier League, can be described for the most part, as a bastion of traditional working-class values and attitudes (Littlewood 2005). Magee (2002) has argued that despite the astronomic rise in players' wages, managers' salaries and the increasing involvement of middle-class professionals in the sport, the culture of professional football remains embedded in the working-class roots of the sport.

According to Littlewood (2005), one of the striking features of certain strands of working-class culture often found in professional football is a suspicion of book learning and academic achievement. Sport psychologists must be prepared to wear their intellectual capabilities and academic knowledge lightly, especially where their ideas challenge rather than confirm those expressed by the manager or coaches.

PSYCHOBABBLE

An accusation frequently charged against psychology is that it is common sense dressed up in obscure and technical language. Within Premier League football clubs this criticism may have been diminished during the past ten years or so, with the significant increase in the employment of sport science and sport medicine staff at clubs. It is not unusual for a Premier League club to have staff with doctorates, master's degrees and undergraduate qualifications. These individuals are themselves familiar with the need to use complex terms, theories and academic models to explain their own activities. This is generally perceived as acceptable since the processes and systems they are describing are generally acknowledged to be highly complex, and requiring specialist knowledge. In contrast, the sport psychologist will refer to motivation, communication skills, relaxation, character and courage – all these terms and many others are used and well understood by everyone, whether or not they are qualified in psychology. This presents the psychologist with a dilemma.

On the one hand they have the benefit of knowing that the people they are working with in the club will already possess a good grasp of many of the concepts and ideas they are referring to. This has been described by Polanyi (1958) in his highly acclaimed and brilliant book on personal knowledge. Here he explains that we know about a vast range of moods, emotions and thoughts because we recognize them in others, having experienced them ourselves in the first place. Polanyi argues that our shared humanness guarantees knowledge about much of the subject matter of psychology. This does not mean that complex technical language is redundant, since this can be useful in adding precision to terms and phrases commonly used, and differentiating clearly between related constructs. This extremely important point seems to have been misunderstood by many psychologists and those who criticize the discipline.

In simple terms, technical language has its place; that place, however, is rarely in one-to-one psychological sessions with players or when talking to the manager about the value of team-building exercises. One of the ways to begin to overcome the fear that is sometimes evident when psychological language *must* be used is to organize a series of continuing professional development (CPD) events in the club at which coaches, the manager and other staff can begin to appreciate that conceptual terms serve a purpose and that they can enhance the accuracy of any assessments or points of discussion.

PHYSICIAN, HEAL THYSELF!

Another difficulty that sometimes confronts the psychologist is there is a widely held view that individuals enter the profession because they are in need of therapy themselves. Within counselling psychology and psychotherapy, there are some approaches that have argued that, in order to be capable of genuine empathy with clients, it is important that the psychologist has suffered from the same problems as the individual they aim to help. From a sport psychology perspective, Andersen (2009) has gone even further, suggesting that many in this profession may need to work through their own psychological issues and crises before they are fit to work with sports performers. The nicknames often directed at sport psychologists working in football nicely capture this particular perspective. 'Shrink', 'psycho', 'wizard' and the 'magician', whilst often said in jest, or even as a term of endearment, reflect a commonly encountered view that psychologists are rather unstable and whimsical individuals, or that they may even be psychologically weak themselves. Within the high achieving and mentally demanding culture of professional and Premier League football, the sport psychologist must be ready to face this challenge.

Another common assumption is that sport psychologists want to help players in order to somehow attempt vicariously to heal their own wounds resulting from failure to become a top performer or professional player. This is pointedly expressed by the question often encountered by sport psychologists in this environment: 'what drove you to want to work as a sport psychologist?' The underlying issue here is neatly captured by the word 'drove'. This seems to imply that sport psychologists are motivated to satisfy some deep-lying and possibly unconscious drives that they are unaware of. I have frequently overheard Premier League players and staff wondering aloud why sport psychologists would choose such a career, unless it was in some way to gain closure for their own disappointments in sport.

20

TIME FAMINE

Nesti and Littlewood (in press) have reported that there has been a substantial increase since the mid-1990s in the numbers of sport science and sport medicine staff working at Premier League clubs. This change has taken place at both academy and first team levels. One of the difficulties arising from this increase is that there are now many more people demanding access to the players on a daily basis. Tactical and technical football-related training heads the queue, most usually followed by medical and physical fitness interventions. Sport psychologists will often struggle to secure a period of time during the player's day at the training ground and will often find themselves having to squeeze their work into unappealing slots in the schedule.

Although experienced sport psychologists such as Andersen (2000) have suggested that much excellent work can be carried out at quick and informal meetings with players or coaches, the fact remains that for more extensive and in-depth support a more formal and lengthy session may be necessary. Although it is possible to deliver this kind of activity beyond the hours that the player is at the training ground, this is increasingly difficult to attain. There are many demands on Premiership footballers such as doing media interviews, community relations work, visiting hospitals and schools. In my experience, only a small number of players are able or willing to commit the necessary time to meet regularly and frequently outside of their normal daily schedule. This often results in the situation where only those with strong organizational skills and self-discipline are prepared to work with the sport psychologist. Whilst this may mean that productive work is possible with these individuals, it may also mean that access to other, and possibly more needy, players is much harder to achieve.

PRIVACY

The issue of confidentiality has been considered by sport psychologists (e.g. Andersen, 2005) working in a wide range of sport settings and environments. Although most professional bodies such as BASES, the BPS Division of Sport and Exercise Psychology (BPSDSEP) and the

American Association of Applied Sport Psychologists (AAASP) provide guidance on confidentiality, there are many differing interpretations of this term in practice. For example, Silva *et al.* (1999) have argued that complete confidentiality between client and psychologist is essential in a sport environment. Nesti (2004) has highlighted, that for some sport psychologists confidentiality often extends beyond work with the individual athlete, and includes those paying for the sport psychology provision in the first place. This could mean that confidentiality really refers to ensuring that only those who directly work with the athlete, such as coaches and other sport scientists, are party to relevant information divulged by the sports performer to the sport psychologist. In my own practice with professional players and within Premiership football clubs I have defined confidentiality in much more strict terms than this, to enable me to carry out my work in a way that is consistent with the theoretical perspectives I use to guide my approach.

Chapter 7 gives a more complete account of why I consider this approach to confidentiality to be *the* central component of the one-to-one work I carry out with players in football. This crucial element of sport psychology work has also been discussed extensively within Nesti (2004) and Nesti and Littlewood (2009). To insist upon such a high level of confidentiality is, in my experience, radically different from the norms governing the practice of other staff within Premier League or other professional football clubs. Given the high profile and valuable resource that staff are working with (i.e. Premiership players), it makes sense that information is shared openly about players between coaches, managers, sport scientists and others in the club. This is another and important way that a multidisciplinary approach to player support can become more fully interdisciplinary. The advantages of utilizing an interdisciplinary approach to work with elite-level sports football players has been discussed by many sport science practitioners. Recent work by Drust *et al.* (2009) within a football context has developed the scope of interdisciplinary work even further by including coaching, paediatric science and body composition, alongside other more traditional sport science and sport medicine disciplines.

Given this commitment to transparency and sharing of information across disciplines, sport psychologists who insist that their work with a player is fully confidential will be operating in a way that may seem to be opposed to interdisciplinary or even multidisciplinary approaches to practice. It is quite understandable how misunderstandings and even distrust can arise in relation to the function and role of the sport psychologist who operates in this way. There will be moments, especially when the team is not performing well, or individual players are suffering a loss of form, where the pressure on the sport psychologist to breach confidentiality will be intense. Again, this is easy to understand in a professional team sport environment where ultimately, failure can result in relegation from the league, huge losses of revenue, and the strong likelihood that the manager, coaches and other staff will lose their jobs.

IMPORTANT BUT UNWELCOME

Finally, it could be argued that many managers, coaches, players and others in Premier League clubs would agree with Pieper (1989) in describing psychology and philosophy as being simultaneously the most useless and the most important subjects. The point being made by Pieper is that for many people, psychology, especially the type that is derived from existential, humanistic and other philosophical foundations, is easy to criticize as something impractical and esoteric. Unlike the work of the coach on the training ground, the fitness staff in the gym, or the physiotherapist in the rehabilitation centre, psychological work lacks a set of easily identifiable outcomes.

Perhaps even worse than this in our increasingly utilitarian and materialist age, psychology, like philosophy, has been poorly received at times because it seems to be about ideas and affecting minds, rather than impacting directly on bodily practice.

Despite these perceptions, many managers, members of the staff team and players recognize that, especially at the highest levels, the mind, mental skills and psychological qualities are the most important components in sustained high-level performance. Ironically, this can lead to genuine frustration about the work of sport psychologists in Premier League football since the expectation of such work may be too idealistic and difficult to carry through effectively, although everyone agrees that even a small change in a player's psychological state can bring significant benefits, or serious problems.

CONCLUSIONS

Sport psychologists need to be cognizant of the particular challenges they will face when working in professional football. Some of these may relate to operational issues and specific practices. These are often quite easy to detect and can be dealt with as the psychologist becomes more familiar with his or her role in a club or with players.

The culture of an organization is in many ways much harder to identify clearly, and can take many years to understand fully. This is because, as Wilson (2001) has claimed, culture captures the values, attitudes and behaviours that underpin organizational practices. These are woven into the fabric of the organization and often evolve over time. In this way culture seems to be ephemeral, easier to 'feel' and sense, than to identify in a precise and tangible fashion.

Sport psychologists can prepare themselves to work in the culture of professional football by attending seminars, conferences and training events where experienced practitioners speak candidly about their work in the game. These need not always be sport psychologists since much can be learned from coaches, other sport science specialists, or players and managers, about the culture that operates in the sport.

They should familiarize themselves with the expanding literature on organizational culture in business (e.g. Wilson 2001) and look beyond the sport psychology peer-reviewed journals towards literature based on sociological, anthropological and philosophical accounts. These studies and articles may be found in a range of peer-reviewed journals, including those that deal with professional sport in business terms, such as the *European Sport Management Quarterly*. There are also some excellent books that will help the sport psychologist to understand more about the culture of professional sport. For example, the work of Gilson *et al.* (2001) on strategy and business practices in some of the world's top sports organizations offers the reader a research-based account dealing with the importance of culture in this environment. Gilmore and Gilson (2007) have also considered the topic of change management within elite sports, which is also related to organizational culture. Finally, Roderick's (2006) account of professional football culture should be essential reading for all sport psychologists who intend to work in this

24

sport in any capacity. Although more sociological than psychological in orientation, this book provides a rich and detailed insider account of the world of professional football. To date, there is nothing in the peer-reviewed journals in sport psychology, or even within the books on sport psychology in football that can offer this level of insight into the culture of the game in the UK.

The sport psychologist should not expect to be able to change this culture easily or quickly. They must attempt to deliver a useful, professional and ethical service within the existing culture. Especially outside of the Premiership, any alteration to culture and organizational practices will usually be a very slow process. The sport psychologist must 'learn the culture' whilst at the same time resist pressures to become assimilated. They will be able to be more effective where they can begin to understand the demands of the culture, without allowing their practices to be compromised excessively by these same demands. This will test their resilience, motivation, values and courage. Many sport psychologists have struggled to deliver what their role demands because of a failure to work with the culture of professional football as opposed to against it. Indeed, some have lost their jobs, or had contracts prematurely terminated, not because of a lack of skill and knowledge in their field, but because they could not 'read' the cultural matrix of professional football and therefore could not adapt to meet its needs.

Sport psychologists who hope to survive and achieve their aims in Premiership and professional football will need to accept that they are being allowed access into a traditionally closed world, one where there is a specific culture that impacts on working practices, social processes and interpersonal relationships, and which often views outsiders as a threat. Becoming a culturally aware sport psychologist in professional football is not about satisfying the demands of political correctness. It is, however, about being able to meet the needs of those you are working with in a climate that is often considerably more challenging and reluctant to embrace sport psychology than most other sports and environments.

ONE-TO-ONE SPORT PSYCHOLOGY COUNSELLING

This chapter looks at the provision of one-to-one sport psychology support with first team Premiership players, young professionals and professional footballers in lower divisions. Within a Premiership club and professional football there are a range of views about the usefulness of sport psychology in helping the team to achieve its aims. As has been discussed in Chapter 1, Premiership football is a fast-paced, unstable and intense environment. Short termism is the order of the day. With each match, clubs have an opportunity to secure vital points in their efforts to qualify for European competitions or avoid relegation. Perceptions of sport psychology in this culture range from acceptance that it must deliver results quickly if it is to be seen as worthwhile, to the more infrequently encountered view that the long-term development of players and teams is something worth waiting for.

The approach that I have taken in my work has most usually involved me in the delivery of organizational psychology work and individually tailored one-to-one sessions for players. Some of the difficulties in providing a series of confidential one-to-one meetings within the club setting have been described by Nesti and Littlewood (2009). The key issues centre on the commitment of the manager to sport psychology provision, the importance of confidentiality, and acceptance that the outcomes of work with players will be difficult to assess relative to other disciplines in sport science. However, one of the most important elements that impacts on the likely success of the sport psychologist in this culture is that of trust. The trust between the manager and the sport psychologist is of great importance. If this is not securely in place, players, coaches and even other support staff may find themselves doubting the value of having a sport psychologist within the team. During periods of success and achievement it is easy to ignore or forget about the importance of trust. However, when the inevitable moments of crises appear, all work at the club will be scrutinized and assessed closely. It is during these moments that the level of trust between the psychologist, staff and players will be most evident.

Teams going through difficult times should focus on factors within their control and on ensuring that both immediate and longer-term goals and tasks are given due consideration. There is little doubt that the best sports organizations and top businesses maintain this type of dual focus during their successful periods, and more importantly, when experiencing more challenging times. The sport psychologist may find that they receive less support to carry out confidential one-to-one work with players during the inevitable tough phases. Such situations, whilst understandable, reveal that it is common to find that the counselling work carried out by the sport psychologist is only fully acceptable in good times. This may lead them to question how fully committed the manager, key staff and players are to their work. Sometimes the players will remain keen to meet with the sport psychologist during challenging moments, even if the manager does not want this to take place. With long-term involvement and a greater understanding about the value of one-to-one work, the sport psychologist should be able to overcome these problems and continue to offer support to the players in good times and bad.

This chapter will also consider the value of using a mental skills training (MST) approach in the delivery of sport psychology to players. This will be contrasted with humanistic and existential phenomenological psychology paradigms (Nesti 2004). In my work I have found that each of these approaches is valuable. Nevertheless, most of my work within the one-to-one confidential sessions with players is guided by existential phenomenological perspectives. These are typically oriented at longer-term change and require the player to actively engage in the process. This approach has been used when delivering work from outside of the club, and also has been helpful in when working from inside a Premiership club. There is little doubt that this approach has been rarely used by sport psychologists during the past forty years. However, highly experienced practitioners such as Ravizza (2002a), Nesti (2004) and Dale (1996) have employed some aspects of this perspective in their support for athletes.

The types of issues faced by the player in Premiership football are similar to those reported by researchers (e.g. Cockerill 2002) working in a range of other high-level team sport environments contexts: deselection from the starting line-up, falling out with the manager or coaching staff, problems relating to motivation, financial matters, competitive anxiety (Jones 1995), existential anxiety (Nesti 2002), knowing and dealing with expectations, and knowing your role and responsibilities on the field of play. These experiences and a number of other challenges are faced by professional football players on a daily, weekly and season-by-season basis. This chapter will describe how these issues are considered and dealt with by the sport psychologist through use of confidential counselling-based sessions.

A further important topic is that of giving accurate, useful and precise information and feedback to the manager and coaching staff emerging from work with players. This is a particularly difficult topic, which must be handled sensitively and with great skill by the sport psychologist. Failure to carry this task out properly, ethically and professionally could quickly lead to the removal of the sport psychologist from the club, or the breakdown in trust with the players. The narrow ridge that must be negotiated between maintaining confidentiality, meeting professional and ethical responsibilities and offering appropriate feedback to parties beyond the counselling sessions, represents one of the hardest tasks facing the sport psychologist.

In my work, unlike that reported by a number of other sport psychologists (e.g. Maynard and Cotton 1993) there is a great reluctance to use psychometric tests, whether sports specific or more general in nature. There are a number of reasons for this that will be examined more closely below. However, this does not mean that it is impossible to identify occasions where such quantitative measures can not prove helpful. For example, the Predictive Index (PI) psychometric personality inventory that I have been trained to use has proved to be an effective tool to enhance a number of aspects of my work with both players and staff. Crucially, this psychometric is oriented at least in part to helping individuals to become more authentic. A major aim of the existential psychology approach is to assist people to accept the responsibility to become more fully themselves, despite the anxiety that may be experienced alongside this process.

Finally, although most counselling-based sessions have taken place in private rooms where confidentiality is easy to guarantee, some of the most powerful encounters have occurred in very different types of locations. For example, dialogue with players may take place in and around the changing room, on the training pitch, in the dining room and even in the showers. As has been previously noted by Andersen (2000), this makes the work of a sport psychologist different from the normal working practices of most other professional psychologists. The data that emerges from these more unplanned, spontaneous and sometimes fleeting sessions may be every bit as important as that emerging from more organized and scheduled meetings. This connects closely to the idea of a holistic approach to sport psychology, and in some ways is closely associated with debate about the value of qualitative and quantitative data (Sparkes 2002).

MENTAL SKILLS TRAINING

It has been observed by many experienced researchers and practitioners in sport psychology (Andersen 2000; Bull *et al.* 1996; Nesti 2007) MST approaches have dominated the provision of sport psychology support across a range of sports. The reasons for this have been detailed extensively in a number of important articles. Arguably, the most erudite and advanced analysis was provided by Corlett's (1996a) work on this topic. His most damming criticism of the discipline was that it has tended to unthinkingly follow the dominant culture prevailing in Western science and culture. Corlett accuses sport psychology of being obsessed with techniques aimed at dealing with symptoms rather than approaches that address the longer-term development of the whole person. He has pointed out that within sport, and especially at high levels of performance, athletes understand that little can be gained easily, quickly and with little apparent effort. In describing much of the cognitive behavioural dominated approach of sport psychology he has accused the discipline of operating like the sophists of ancient

Greece. These individuals were able to live financially and materially comfortable lives by teaching the skills that were considered essential to allow young ambitious individuals, in particular, to acquire power and influence within the establishment in Athenian society. Although not directly referring to sport, the idea that Corlett (1996a) is attempting to explain is that quick fix and easy-to-learn mental skills can bring some success immediately. However, against this, there should be a recognition that the most secure and important development of the individual can only take place through developing their self-knowledge. As Corlett has pointed out, this takes great effort and time, and can never be a completed task. Sport psychologists adopting this philosophy of practice (Lindsay *et al.* 2007) may be comfortable teaching imagery skills, self-talk and relaxation strategies; the most important focus of their work, however, would be on encouraging athletes to know themselves more fully.

PHILOSOPHICAL GROUNDING

My approach to practice is grounded in my undergraduate and postgraduate education, and, importantly, has been supplemented by continual reading of psychological and more philosophically grounded work over the past twenty years of applied practice. The types of articles and books that I have been most interested in are often from areas outside sport and sport psychology. Literature from psychotherapy, counselling psychology, philosophy and even theology have helped me to develop a philosophical underpinning to my psychological practice. The most useful approaches for my work have emanated from humanistic, gestalt, existential and other person-centred perspectives (Caruso 1964; May 1977). The philosophical tradition located within the work of Pieper (1989), Buber (1958), Chesterton (1993), and the theological work of Aquinas (1964) has allowed me to study ideas that are beyond the philosophical dualism that has dominated Western thinking and science for the past 400 years. These writers and thinkers alongside the work of phenomenologists such as Giorgi (1970) have linked to the existential psychology of Van Kamm (1969) and the earlier foundational work of Kierkegaard (1944 [1844]).

Taken together, of this body of work has a common thread. It conceives of human persons holistically; that is, being made up of mind, body and spirit. These approaches reject the validity of a 'scientific' approach to psychology, that is, one that can only conceive of reality in terms of the cannons of the natural sciences. In other words, this rejects a psychology that does not accept anything unless it can be measured and evaluated according to rigorous scientific method. At the same time, these approaches avoid the weakness of the opposing view that only subjective experiences are worthy of study. Their solution to the one-sided, positivist, reductionist approach of scientific psychology is not to replace it with an equally one-sided perspective based purely on feelings, emotions and other subjective states. The starting point for any work or research by the above-mentioned writers is based on the most important empirical data available to us. *This data emerges directly from the description of events and circumstances of our lives.* These are not reduced to cause-and-effect type relationships and neither are they conceived as merely perceptions. Human thought and emotion is considered to be part of one inseparable process.

In terms of helping my own learning and reflection this literature has offered an appealing synthesis that offers a robust philosophical base to my activities. If this appears to be a long way from doing applied sport psychology in professional football, then a recent paper by Lindsay *et al.* (2007) suggests that this is in fact not the case. They have argued convincingly that in order to effectively deliver sport psychology, there needs to be congruence between the philosophy of practice and the personal philosophy of the psychologist. Although I agree with this stress on the importance of congruency and authenticity in practice, and the emphasis on the importance of philosophy to psychology, their work fails to identify *which* philosophical perspective is the most useful and necessary. Another way of expressing this is that there is a need to ground our psychological practice in philosophical perspectives that are consistent with important and well-meaning statements, such as Martens's (1987) earlier call that sport psychologists should work with the person first and the athlete second.

PUTTING IT INTO PRACTICE

The following semi-fictional accounts are based on the typical sessions that I have been able to deliver on a weekly basis whilst working within Premiership clubs and with professional footballers. The majority of encounters took place in a private office space at the clubs' training grounds.

During the meetings we were attempting to continue work on the issues that had been identified as important to the players' match performances, and much time was devoted to considering what they planned to do in the future to improve these.

I often ask the player for his reflections on what we had covered at our last session, and to help this process, I usually provided him with a further copy of the brief report sent after our meeting. In my experience, some players read this material carefully whilst others seem satisfied not to engage in reflections based on written accounts. Over the years I have carefully tailored the language, format and length of my reports to meet the needs of the player to ensure that they benefit from this piece of work. There is a great variety of responses to the written word, and some players have informed me that they would prefer to have briefer notes provided after meetings to remind them of what has been discussed. Other players have reacted positively to 1,500-word reports which they not infrequently share with significant others, such as wives, family and agents. The sport psychologist also benefits in that the reports provide a detailed account of what was discussed with the player, and they can be used to check progress.

The topic of providing written feedback to athletes working with sport psychologists has been infrequently addressed in the sport psychology literature. However, some highly experienced applied sport psychologists have a positive view about the value of getting athletes to write reports, although this is usually outside elite professional team sports environments (personal communication). One of the great challenges in an elite professional sports environment like Premiership football is to get players to write things down. In most cases this is not how they have learned their sport, and is often perceived negatively. Where I have attempted to get players to engage in even modest amounts of writing there has been a great reluctance to be involved. Younger players in academy settings and even some young professionals are more willing to engage in this task, however, generally speaking, writing is viewed as something rather academic and detached from the learning experiences of professional footballers.

At the start of one meeting with a player we talked about the difficult period that the team had been experiencing in the previous five matches. During this time we had fallen out of the top eight sides in the league and were now close to the relegation zone. The player had played in four of these games and had occupied three different positions.

We turned to the goals that they had set for themselves earlier on in the season. Some of these referred to a number of appearances that they hoped to achieve, goals scored and minutes played. From a more process goal perspective, this particular player identified a need to improve their first touch, short passing and ability to react well to mistakes. In addition to this we had been working on a greater use of imagery skills as part of their pre-performance routines (Williams 2006). The sport psychology literature (Goldberg 1998; Orlick 2000) often conveys an impression that few athletes use visualization, mental rehearsal, positive self-talk, or pre-performance routines as part of their psychological preparation. In my experience it is extremely rare to come across any player, especially in Premiership football, who is not using some if not all of these mental skills. The opportunity to deliver work in relation to these types of mental skills is often only possible on occasions where they are not being used as perfectly, or effectively, as possible. On other occasions it may be that small adjustments are necessary to 'freshen up' and sharpen existing mental skills. In my experience, only on rare occasions will it be necessary to teach a completely new set of mental skills to a Premiership player, or high-level professional footballer. This is quite logical given that to achieve at this level of performance a player must already possess excellent mental skills. This has been reported by Murphy and White (1995) and Gould *et al.* (2002) when discussing Olympic-level athletes. Unfortunately, this important piece of information seems frequently to be forgotten, or may be even ignored, by those sport psychologists who claim that their most important role is to teach MST to all levels of sports performers.

My work with Premiership players, as with my experience with high-level racing drivers, swimmers, tennis players, cricketers and golfers, is that mental skills training represents a small part of any work with them. Nesti (2004) has pointed out that this situation has been a problem for many years in the training and education of sport psychologists especially where they expect to work with elite-level performers. Some of the reasons for this relate to how educational programmes often lack awareness of other approaches in psychology beyond the cognitive and behavioural. Other reasons could be that many sport psychologists have not been exposed to theoretical approaches that closely examine the notion of personal identity in sport.

Self-knowledge and identity

Much that takes place in a counselling session with elite-level sport performers involves players looking closely at their identity. The topic of identity has been studied in sport psychology, although rarely from anything other than a trait-based approach that relies on psychological inventories to measure athletic identity (e.g. Brewer *et al.* 1993). This research has investigated the influence of having a strong athletic identity on a number of psychological factors in young athletes in particular. With high-level professional athletes such as Premiership footballers, athletic identity has not been a useful construct in guiding my applied work. Players tend to view themselves as being both professional athletes and persons who must live a life not solely dictated by their vocational status as Premiership or professional footballers. The separation between athletic identity and their identity as individuals living in broader society is not something I have encountered often in my work at this level. In contrast, the existential psychology account of identity describes this concept in terms of meaning. Maslow (1968) commended the existential perspective for being the first approach in psychology to provide a more precise and empirical account of identity. He was in agreement with existential psychologists who claimed that our identity rests on the meaning we ascribe to events, situations and people we encounter across our lives. The existential view ranges from those who suggest that the most important task facing people is to discover meaning in our lives to those who argue that we have a responsibility to create meaning (Sartre 1958). Frankl (1984) went further than some of his existentially minded colleagues and claimed that our most important task is to discover an ultimate source of meaning and values that can provide a constant guide and anchor for individuals. His approach is referred to as logo therapy, and it emerged after his experiences as a physician suffering incarceration in a concentration camp for three years during the Second World War. This may seem to be a great distance from the world of sport psychology and professional football, given the horror and tragic events that Frankl lived through. However, his message was that irrespective of the environment and its difficulties and challenges, our capacity to withstand the pressures and crushing stress we may face is related to the possession of deeply held values that have been won personally. According to his views, the greatest need for human beings to survive and flourish is to be able to locate their identity within a nexus of values and beliefs that are connected to something bigger than the self. Clearly, Frankl is referring to spiritual and religious belief, as well as other belief systems, that are not tied to immediate gain or self-gratification.

In sessions with Premiership players dealing with self-confidence and doubt, these issues have emerged and been used to shape discussions. The Premiership is a remarkably multicultural environment, at least as far as players are concerned. Many of these individuals possess strong spiritual and religious beliefs that are the most important factor in their identity as people. Time and again, Premiership players, especially those from outside the UK, have mentioned that the meaning that they are able to secure from these beliefs and their faith help them to deal with the many moments where they and others doubt their ability and undermine their confidence. As has been explained by Nesti (2007) and Watson and Nesti (2005), the education and research paradigms that have dominated sport psychology do not adequately prepare sport psychologists to deal with these topics when they emerge from their clients. This is not a matter of whether the sport psychologist is religiously minded, or subscribes to a set of spiritual beliefs. Rather, it is a question of how the sport psychologist should address these issues with sensitivity and insight. This is because the person sitting opposite is informing the sport psychologist that these sources of meaning are central to who they are and how they deal with the achievements and failures of their professional and personal lives.

The Premiership player discussing self-confidence rarely remains at the level of cognitive or behavioural constructs. Self-confidence is something that they understand since they have been in a situation where this has been repeatedly tested and assailed from without. Even when a player is satisfied with his own performance, there may be negative and destructive reports in the media, or from the manager, coaching staff and other key individuals. This could be because the player is not liked by the club because of rumours about his intention to leave for another club at the end of the season, or because he is a strong character who expresses unpopular opinions in the changing room, or on the training ground. The term mental toughness has been studied from 2000–2009 within the sport psychology literature. Although there may be many interesting questions that remain unanswered about this construct (Crust 2007), there seems to be an excellent understanding of this concept within Premiership football.

A counselling session with the player hoping to address self-confidence often deals with other closely related topics beyond the matter of identity and meaning. The player will often talk about how crucial it is that they remain committed to the work they know they must do to develop themselves, and recognize that they must not get distracted and focus should be on factors within their control where possible. These elements have been identified by Crust (2007) and others as being central to ideas related to mental toughness. The sport psychologist in this situation has an opportunity to delve deeper into each of these and ensure that the player is fully aware of what they need to address these. It is often important that they ensure that the player is not attempting to take on too much. Because professional footballers and Premiership players are often highly motivated and determined individuals, they have a tendency to be over-critical of themselves and to try too hard as they work on building their confidence again. This task of confronting the player with the choices they intend to make is often an uncomfortable experience for both the psychologist and the athlete.

It can sometimes appear to players that the sport psychologist is attempting to hold them back whilst on other occasions they may feel that they are being provoked to push themselves a little further, or faster, than they would have gone alone. These moments in the encounter can lead to a dialogue infused with passion and emotion. The existential view is one of the only perspectives in psychology that is positive about this form of dialogue. The aim is to speak in a direct and clear way, without using technical language that could obscure the matter at hand. Again, it is not considered a problem if there is a high degree of spontaneity, and if both parties speak to one another in a relatively unguarded and intense way. The idea behind this is that if the session is discussing something important and real in someone's life, then the communication both in style and substance should be up to the task. Dispassionate, disengaged analytical thinking is required from the sport psychologist during the session and most certainly afterwards, when any notes are written up. This does not mean that the sport psychologist should engage in a close and emotional unstructured conversation – the session is not meant to be a meeting of friends, but is intended to be an opportunity for a successful athlete (a Premiership footballer) to be courageous enough to undergo an intense examination of his or her confidence and its relationship to who they are and what they wish to be.

This approach has been discussed in Buber's (1958) work, which has been described as one of the most profound and important books of the twentieth century in the areas of psychotherapy, education and psychology. Buber's notion of the *I thou* dialogue, which refers to a situation in which two individuals meet in a moment of 'pure' communication, is something that I have found remarkably useful in my work with elite sport performers, including Premiership football players. His work emphasizes that our task as sport psychologists is in many ways little different from others engaged in helping people to become more fully themselves. The notion of authenticity links into this idea. Nesti (2004) has argued that top-level sport performers are often clear about what they stand for and who they are, which in turn allows them to be themselves, that is, authentic, on many more occasions than other sport performers at lower levels. Working with a Premiership player on the notion of authenticity is not about establishing a prescriptive plan, or identifying a strategy beforehand. This project is one that can never be fully completed and is something that can only be achieved and pursued by the players themselves in their own unique ways.

38

PERFORMANCE OR PERSONAL AGENDA?

At the elite level, especially beyond youth sport levels, it is usual to find that most players already possess excellent mental skills. As has been reported by researchers investigating a number of other sports (Gould *et al.* 2002), high-level sport performers have usually acquired solid skills in relation to concentration, maintaining confidence, the use of imagery and goal-setting. This has taken place after guidance from coaches and on occasion from sport psychologists; often it is something that has been learned by the individual themselves as they have progressed through the competitive sport environment. Several researchers and practitioners (Andersen 2005; Nesti 2004) have discussed whether mental skills training is *fit for purpose*. They have argued that much of their work, especially with high-performing athletes, centres on the development of other personal qualities and dealing with broader life issues and concerns.

Mental skills training is clearly performance-focused, and in working as a sport psychologist in professional football it is essential to remember that the main task of the psychologist is to enhance performance. Some psychologists have argued that this performance focus is a hostage to fortune (Andersen 2009; Andersen and Tod 2006) because the psychologist is incapable of clearly demonstrating how their interventions directly improve outcome and competitive results. Some, such as Gilbourne and Richardson (2006), have suggested that sport psychologists should provide more of a caring support role, and that this is where most legitimate activity would lie with teams and individual sports performers. Watson and Nesti (2005) have challenged both these views and argue that sport psychologists should be able to provide mental skills training, performance-focused interventions, as well as support that seems more aligned to approaches adapted from within counselling psychology. Nesti and Littlewood (in press) point out that in practice many of the concerns dealt with by sport psychologists relating to the sport performer's life outside competitive sport – for example, relationships with coaches, position within the team and other less immediately performance-focused topics – can be more influential on the achievement level that the player attains than concerns within the sport itself.

To summarize, the argument seems to be that sport psychologists must choose between two mutually exclusive options. In the first of these they should attend only to a narrow range of psychological skills that directly relate to performance on the field of play or at the training ground. The other choice is to provide a skilled level of professional social support aimed at ensuring athletes can manage their lifestyle and emotions within their existence as professional football players. Especially at elite levels of performance, this option to choose one form of support in preference to another rarely exists in practice, since clubs employ sport psychologists primarily to help players improve performances.

Athletes and sport psychologists, irrespective of approach, will be unable to do useful and meaningful work together without developing trust and a strong working relationship. This means that the work between both parties will involve a personal dimension. This should not be mistaken for friendship, or used to suggest that the role is only about caring and individual support. This seems to be a misunderstood aspect of sport psychology practice, although within the more established fields of psychotherapy and counselling psychology much has been written on the importance of this facet in psychological work. Within some traditions, notably humanistic and existential, the relationship between the therapist and their client has actually been referred to as the most important element within any work that is taking place. Drawing on Buber (1958), Nesti (2007) has pointed out that the capacity for a dialogue to develop in the first place, and for this to have a positive effect on the athlete, depends largely on the personal qualities of the psychologist. Through the use of an *encounter* the psychologist and the athlete engage in an intense and authentic mode of communication. In this situation there are no topics or issues that cannot be brought to the discussion. This does not mean that the sport psychologist is expected or required to deal with clinical issues that may be presented by the athlete. However, it does mean that everything else that makes up the total identity of the sports performer should be on the table for discussion. At conference presentations in Europe and North America, it is common to hear the most experienced and skilled sport psychology practitioners talking about the need to view the athlete they are working with as a person first and a sports performer second. If this means anything, it must mean that in working with this individual the sport psychologist will listen to everything that the athlete considers to be important to his or her likelihood of success. In my experience with high-level professional footballers, rarely does this mean that discussions focus exclusively on developing better mental preparation routines, self-talk strategies and relaxation techniques. Much more time is devoted to listening to athletes discussing their understanding of who they are, how people see them, and how they sustain themselves as a person required to repeatedly deliver exceptional performances week after week over many seasons. If this description sounds closely related to philosophy then this is as it should be! Psychology has its roots in philosophy, and some have argued that sport psychologists need to understand the philosophical underpinnings of the approaches they use to ensure congruence between their own work and the needs of the sports performer (Lindsay *et al.* 2007). Unfortunately, due to a number of historical pressures and the education and training of many within sport psychology until recently, the approach taken to sport psychology work with performers has relied almost exclusively on cognitive behavioural interventions that are philosophically grounded in a natural science paradigm. These approaches have emerged from the laboratory, or are from a positivist research tradition.

As discussed in previous literature (Nesti 2004, 2007) the existential phenomenological approach to psychology that partly informs my own work is in fact deeply opposed to the use of techniques within work between psychologist and client. This approach sometimes even rejects the validity of using counselling skills within an encounter with a client. The complex but important reasons behind this relate to ensuring that the sports performer is viewed as a person who plays sport and not solely as a sport performer. The existential phenomenological approaches insist that the psychologist does all that they can to avoid using technical and psychological terminology within sessions. This often helps put the performer at ease. The language used is essentially the same as would take place in a normal conversation. In other words, through considering the culture, experience and educational level of the athlete, the sport psychologist will adjust to ensure that both parties can converse freely and comfortably. Because of this, the best sessions frequently resemble an intense and focused conversation. The sport psychologist must guide this dialogue; his key task is to ensure that issues and factors are clarified and confronted. To many less experienced sport psychologists this sounds like the description of two friends having a conversation. However, this is a misunderstanding because the encounter has a clear aim (i.e. clarification), is often uncomfortable, may have a directive element and is oriented towards helping someone to improve their sports performance. Dialogue, encounter and meeting are terms written about extensively within counselling psychology and psychotherapy, especially from humanistic and existential perspectives.

Using this approach allows the professional footballer to be able to engage without the distraction of feeling that they are being analysed or instructed in new ways of mentally preparing. During some sessions it has been within the first five minutes that the footballer has decided to look at topics such as leaving the club, refusing to go on loan, discussing the perceived corruption surrounding the selection and transfer of players, or any other often controversial and deeply complex issue that they are concerned about. This is no mere conversation, however, between two acquaintances who care about one another. The skill is in ensuring that the player is always attuned to the fact that a wide range of matters is being discussed so that they can be dealt with, clarified or brought into awareness to enable the athlete to perform better as a professional player. Many of these topics sound like the sorts of things that a player might discuss with an agent, family, friends or others. However, there is a crucial difference here. These topics are not being shared with the sport psychologist in order to attain merely some kind of emotional support, but are divulged in anticipation that, through the application of psychological knowledge, it will be possible to deal constructively with these matters to ensure that they do not provide an obstacle to the further achievement of the player. This narrow ridge between engaging in an intimate level of conversation as one would see between close friends, and maintaining some necessary degree of professional distance has been richly described by Buber (1958). He makes the point that for this type of work to succeed, the therapist or psychologist must approach the other as a person and view them with the respect that they deserve as a fellow human being. However, he warns that a distance must be maintained to ensure that the educative process remains possible. Buber has pointed out that the relationship between the teacher and pupil, the medical doctor and patient, or the

42

priest and the penitent will lose its educative power if the inclusion is total. The need to maintain a point of difference means that the sessions usually have a slight air of tension and anxiety. The existential view contends that this form of anxiety is potentially constructive since it ensures that the individual is energized to confront their challenges. It is by considering and facing up to the tasks and challenges that the athlete will develop self-knowledge and become a stronger person. This cannot be acquired easily, although during the many challenges and difficulties encountered in any professional sports career there are ample opportunities to develop these personal qualities without the support of a sport psychologist. However, sometimes help is needed to accelerate this growth, or when an athlete has lost their way. It is particularly at boundary situations or critical moments (Nesti and Littlewood 2009) where professional footballers face important changes in their career, performance and ultimately identity, that the opportunity presents itself. At these moments the sport psychologist adopting this approach could prove particularly useful in assisting the athlete to accept that they are responsible for their development towards self-knowledge, self-actualization (Maslow 1968) or authenticity (May 1977).

LIVING ENCOUNTERS

In order to explain more fully how this takes place in a sport psychology counselling session with a Premiership footballer it may be useful to look more closely at some of the most frequently occurring matters that emerge during encounters. The first of these relates to dealing with selection and deselection. There are no players who play every match in first team football throughout their careers. Whether this means that they are coming back from injury, have been suspended, or have lost form, this experience is part and parcel of the life of a top class professional footballer. This may be very different from the experience that they have had progressing through youth levels of sport. Typically, Premiership players have been outstanding young performers and have rarely been dropped from their age group teams. Within the first team Premiership environment where squads can easily be made up of twenty-five to thirty players, the competition for places is incredibly intense. Premiership footballers know that they can take nothing for granted regarding their place in the team. Sometimes the sport psychologist dealing with this topic will discover that the athlete has forgotten to use particular psychological skills that have helped them in the past, or they may even on occasion need to acquire and learn new techniques that will help. I have spoken to players who have become careless with their pre-performance routines, or have allowed negative visualization to become a part of their pre-match routine. These and other more mental skill problems can be addressed within the sessions with the sport psychologist, and will even be more effective if supported by the manager and coaches where appropriate.

However, I have worked with players over several seasons where the key topic has been related to managing the process of deselection from the first team and the impact this has on identity. Given the high profile and intensive media scrutiny of Premiership players, as well as the particular cultural pressures associated with operating within high achieving environments, it is little wonder that for many players their identity is disrupted during these situations. An existential psychology perspective argues that these disruptions are potential opportunities to develop greater self-knowledge leading to more psychological strength and character in the player.

Corlett (1996b) in drawing on the work of St Thomas Aquinas, Aristotle and others, has pointed out that the quality of courage is something necessary to the continual achievement of high-level sport performers. When a player, especially in first team environments, has been dropped from the starting 11 or the squad, they face a difficult task for a number of reasons. This is not a matter of merely resetting goals and attempting to maintain a positive outlook. Usually the player will have to deal with the media coverage surrounding their deselection and may also have to face questions from their agents, advisors and family and friends about the situation. The usual response of the latter is to provide well-meaning but often impractical advice for the player.

The management and coaching team within the club could have withdrawn the player for a large number of reasons. This could be for tactical advantage, or maybe because of a perceived lack of form, or because objective performance statistics have identified that the player is physically or technically deficient. There are also situations where the reasons are more personal and relate to disagreements between manager, coaches and the player about their behaviour. This could be to do with their attitude and communication with peers around the training ground, or equally, something to do with their behaviour in their broader lives. It is a common mistake in much of the literature in sport psychology to imagine that this refers to clinical issues, or significant problems such as drug taking, alcohol abuse or other similar types of activities. Often, the difficulties that the player faces are about more mundane but nevertheless important matters. It could be, for example, that a manager drops a player because he believes he is distracted as a result of relationship problems at home, or because his children have been unable to settle in a new area and at a new school. It has been well supported by many experienced practitioners (Murphy and White 1995) that at the highest level very small differences can have important consequences. The sport psychologist working with the deselected player is required to examine the situation surrounding the player's non-participation in the team and to begin to identify possible solutions where these exist. Sometimes the course of action may involve addressing a number of capacities that are to some degree in the control of the player. For example, it may be that additional weight training, a change in diet, or ensuring that more high intensive sprint activities are demonstrated in competitive matches by the individual. Beyond being able to begin to address some of these difficulties, the most challenging aspect in elite professional football is where the player is unable to clearly identify the reason for his deselection. In my experience there is great variation in the explanations and information divulged to the player about the reasons that they are not in the team. This presents both an opportunity for the player as well as being a great source of frustration and even anger.

Much of the time the only available constructive response from the player is to engage in a process of deep reflection and self-analysis. The sport psychologist must help the player to examine his overall performances, behaviours, mentality and how this is perceived by the manager and other key members of staff. This requires courage because the player is involved in a process of exploring where he feels he could make positive changes in his football life, and broader life in general.

The sport psychologist must attempt to guide this dialogue to ensure that the player considers his choices and decisions and accepts the responsibility to act on these. Without always having all the necessary information available (notably, that from the coaches and the manager), the player nevertheless must attend to every aspect of himself in an effort to work towards improvement, no matter how small this may seem. For some individuals this task is too difficult to carry out. They may hope that the sport psychologist will provide the answers they are looking for. In my experience, most Premiership footballers do not expect or want this kind of overly directive support. They are generally acutely aware that the most lasting form of learning originates with themselves. At this crucial stage in the encounter, the sport psychologist must take great care to avoid easing the anxiety, uncomfortable feelings and frustration that the player may be feeling. The existential psychology approach is less interested in making people feel 'good' and is more oriented towards helping people to fulfil themselves (Nesti 2007). As has been previously explained, fulfilment in this sense is based on authenticity.

Emotions relating to a player's deselection are always intense. These feelings can lead to an undermining of confidence and motivation. The existential approach recognizes that feelings have the potential to be constructive or negative. However, unlike most other approaches, it contends that a level of discomfort, suffering and anxiety is most usually felt during periods of change and growth (Nesti and Littlewood 2009).

The sport psychologist and the player must attempt to ignore the desire to deal with the symptoms first, and they should scrutinize the situation to, at the very least, throw some light on the possible causes of the problem. Deselection is something that all professional footballers experience without exception. It usually causes anxiety and distress for the player. The issue of mental toughness has been described by several researchers as one of the key elements associated with successful sports performers (Jones *et al.* 2002). Whilst this term has been usefully defined and measured in sport psychology (Clough *et al.* 2002), there are few better examples of where it is more necessary than when having to deal with being dropped from the team. The self-image and professional pride of the player is put under considerable pressure by this event.

It is important from an existential psychology perspective that the sport psychologist does not attempt to suggest tactical or technical reasons that have led to this situation (although where the psychologist works closely with the manager and coaches, the player will be aware that the psychologist may have detailed knowledge about some of the reasons why the player has not been chosen). The player will usually understand that confidentiality must exist both between himself and the sport psychologist, and between the sport psychologist and the manager. In my experience few players directly question the psychologist about what they have heard from the manager about any decisions affecting the football club. Selection for teams is one area where players would not expect the manager to divulge the full reasons to any staff apart from the assistant manager and possibly first team coach. This ensures that the manager in a Premiership club is able to make decisions for the good of the team without being unduly concerned about the difficulties that these decisions may bring to individual players. The same is true of other team sports. However, with the intense media scrutiny and huge public interest in finding out who will start in the first 11 in Premiership teams and professional football clubs, it would be unrealistic to expect detailed explanations for the exclusion relating to what can sometimes be another twenty players who have not been picked to start.

One of the most frequent situations in such a demanding environment as Premier League football is where a player loses confidence in their performances. The need to perform at your best levels, week in, week out, over a period of nine and a half months can place a huge strain on the players. Although there appear to be some individuals who rarely experience problems with confidence, this is not the case for the majority. The cliché in football is that confidence is ultimately based on results. The obvious difficulty with this formula revolves around the fact that each week at least half of the teams in the division do not get the result they are looking for! If results go against a team for a short period of time in the Premier League or elite professional football, a team can quickly find itself in trouble at the wrong end of the division. Although individual players within the team may be performing well, confidence will be greatly affected by league position, negative media coverage and the criticism of fans and others involved in the game.

Most top players at this level are, in my experience of working with them, aware that confidence must be placed on stronger foundations than merely being related to the result of the team. Within the sport psychology literature there has been a rather academic and somewhat arcane debate about what has been referred to as task and ego orientation. Extensive research by Duda *et al.* (1995) has suggested that a task orientation, where the focus is on performance rather than results and outcome, is the best situation for both enjoyment and performance. Others, such as Hardy (1997), have challenged this in claiming that both a task and ego orientation are necessary, and that there is evidence that those who remain committed to sport and perform at the highest levels possess both forms. In my sport psychology encounters with Premier League footballers the most common situation is one where players possess strong ego orientations and an equally strong task orientation. They are aware that both are central to why they are involved in professional football and that these orientations can compliment one another *where they are kept in some form of balance.* They are equally aware that given the pressures and profile associated with the sport, that the ego orientation must be kept in its place and that they must constantly devote their energies to the process goals that are the basis of their professional career and achievement.

The existential psychology approach to anxiety differs markedly from the dominant cognitive psychology perspective in sport psychology. For an established Premiership player to discuss an issue like that of self-confidence requires courage and a high level of self-awareness on behalf of the individual. It is rare for someone to merely bleat out that, despite appearances to the contrary, they are riddled with anxiety, self-doubt and low self-esteem. These concepts are always difficult to talk about because they focus on the self, that is, our psychological core, or identity.

Following the phenomenological approach used in an existential encounter, there is an attempt to get the player to describe in as much detail as possible what it *feels* like to experience a lack of self-confidence, and to examine this in detail *without attempting to suggest reasons for its occurrence.* This is a difficult enterprise since it goes against our natural attitude (Giorgi 1970), which is to attempt to explain why something is experienced, or takes place, often before a thorough and rigorous description has been provided.

48

Finally, existential psychology considers the experience of anxiety to be something that is a constant throughout our lives. Anxiety is seen as something that can be constructive and is something that often accompanies periods of growth and change. Referred to as normal anxiety (May 1995), the existential approach to anxiety is the earliest and most scholarly account of this important human phenomenon (Fischer 1970). When working with a professional football player discussing their deepest self, or to phrase it somewhat differently their identity, the discussion is rarely able to proceed easily and smoothly. For a player to engage in looking closely at who they are, takes great courage and self-discipline. The role of the sport psychologist is to help the individual to clarify who and what they are, in order that they can make choices about whom and what they hope to become. This task is always infused with normal anxiety. Despite being uncomfortable, the existential psychology view is that this *normal anxiety* in itself can be viewed as something positive. Indeed, the founder of existentialism (Kierkegaard 1944 [1844]) famously stated that, 'the greater the self, the greater the anxiety!' This can be interpreted to mean that the more a person grows, develops and becomes fully themselves (i.e. authentic), the more anxiety they will encounter along the way. The sport psychologist's job is to accompany the player in their journey towards fulfilling their potential. This will involve facing up to the anxiety of choice and decision. Ultimately, this can only be done by players themselves, although the presence of the sport psychologist in an encounter can provide important support for this process of honest and courageous self-analysis to take place.

SUPPORTING THE COACHING TEAM AND DEVELOPING THE STAFF

THE SPORT PSYCHOLOGIST AS AN ORGANIZATIONAL PSYCHOLOGIST/HUMAN RESOURCE MANAGER

Although this chapter is concerned with the coaching team, as the title suggests, it would be more accurate to state that the sport psychologist should seek to work with all members of the backroom staff irrespective of their role with the team. This group would typically include the manager, the assistant manager, first team coach, reserve team manager and goalkeeping coach. In addition, some of this work can extend to providing support and guidance to sport science related staff, such as those involved in performance analysis, strength and conditioning, fitness, medical and physiotherapy provision and scouting. In some cases the youth development coaching team, or academy staff, could also be another group that could benefit from this type of activity.

Staff numbers in Premiership clubs have grown significantly since the inception of the league in 1992. It is now common for clubs to have a sport science and medical staff of ten, fifteen or more full-time and part-time individuals. The number of full-time coaches can range from six or seven people working with the first team, and to sometimes up to 10 staff supporting academy-level operations. Although within professional football the coaching and management role is well established and understood, collaboration with fellow team-members in the broad area of sport science and sport medicine is a relatively new phenomenon. Taken as a whole between first team and Academy levels, especially at more established Premier League clubs, there may be upwards of between forty to fifty staff operating in full-time and part-time roles across all of these functions.

This chapter will examine how the sport psychologist in this environment will often function like an organizational psychologist or human resource manager. Amongst other tasks, this will involve them in designing and implementing a system of professional and personal support for the backroom staff. This could involve writing job descriptions, establishing appraisal mechanisms, running staff away days, offering continuing professional development sessions (CPD), and generally supporting the personal development and training opportunities of all of the backroom team. In ordinary medium- to large-scale organizations outside sport, these types of tasks are most usually carried out by individuals with professional qualifications in human resource management and personnel. At lower levels of professional football and in many other less wealthy sports, it is unusual to have staff numbers that are so great they require this type of support.

Within Olympic and national teams, the numbers of specialist staff can be equal to, and in some cases greater than, those found in most Premiership clubs. In recent years much of the task of organizing the processes associated with good communication between different departments, and developing strategy and policy for the sports organization, has been taken on by performance directors. Although many of these individuals are former coaches, an increasing number have a background in business management or organizational psychology. Somewhat surprisingly, very few have emerged directly from the world of human resource management. Some of the reasons for this situation are related to the idiosyncratic nature of professional sport, difficulties associated with access to this environment and a lack of appreciation of the need for such individuals.

The sport psychologist may be rather surprised to find that, alongside an expectation that they will work closely with players to enhance their psychological skills and qualities, they will usually be identified as the most appropriate person to take on this hybrid role of organizational psychologist/human resource manager.

This chapter will consider the skills and personal qualities that may be considered necessary to succeed in pursuing this role within the context of professional sport and Premiership football in particular. Some sport psychologists have had previous experience of delivering this type of support, and may even possess qualifications that will assist them in carrying out these duties. However, as has been pointed out by Nesti (2004) and Lindsay *et al.* (2007), the tendency of most of university-based sport psychology programmes to concentrate on mental skills training and literature that focuses on quantitative group-based research designs investigating a range of emotions inadequately prepares individuals who find themselves charged with delivering an organizational psychology role.

Within this chapter there will be an attempt to consider how sport psychologists can still achieve much despite lacking the formal qualifications to do this type of work. The question remains as to why clubs are reluctant to employ individuals who have previous experience of delivering this kind of support in commercial or public service organizations. Arguably, the most important reason is that there is usually little awareness within the football club of the need for this kind of work until the sport psychologist is invited to join the backroom staff. This paradox occurs because of a number of reasons. One likely explanation is that amongst the coaching and management team of a Premiership club there are usually few individuals who have worked in environments outside professional football. As a consequence of this, they may not have prior knowledge of the kinds of work that are carried out by individuals in other work or business settings that could prove useful in football clubs.

In terms of the specific tasks that the sport psychologist can engage in within this role, the following, whilst not intending to be an exhaustive list, is offered as a possibility. The use of psychometric personality tests that allow the sport psychologist to enhance communication between individuals and assist the development of staff in relation to their professional roles could be a useful tool in this setting. It is common practice in many business organizations to use psychometric testing as part of a recruitment process and to employ this device in a skilful and sensitive way to assist staff development. Although unusual within a Premiership football club, there are examples of good practice involving use of such tests. These will be discussed briefly within this chapter.

An important ingredient that the sport psychologist can add is to encourage staff to enhance their skills and professional knowledge through engaging in CPD. A sport psychologist may decide to offer a CPD programme within the confines of the club, delivered by staff in multi- and interdisciplinary settings. As an alternative, CPD opportunities could involve attendance at workshops and courses outside the club. These can serve to motivate staff in their existing roles and lead to new ideas and more effective ways of working. In addition, staff may benefit from advice on career development opportunities and other educational courses, especially where the sport psychologist is based part time in the club and has strong links with universities and other institutions of higher education.

The sport psychologist will often discover that staff do not possess job descriptions, and where they do, these are often very basic. Working closely with individuals with the support of the manager to devise detailed job descriptions can bring clarification to roles and help avoid communication problems and other inefficiencies. It is also a vehicle through which a system of regular appraisals can be put in place. This is common practice in most public and private organizations outside professional sport and Premiership football. It can become an invigorating and stimulating addition to the more informal feedback mechanisms already in place.

The sport psychologist may also adopt a mentorship role, especially with new, inexperienced or recently qualified staff. This is particularly powerful where the sport psychologist has considerable experience of high-level professional sport and professional football in particular. The sport psychologist may be able to mentor less experienced, newly appointed staff who are involved in delivering sport psychology programmes at academy levels, or with very young players and their parents. Additionally, the sport psychologist might offer confidential one-to-one counselling for the staff. This could be oriented to assist staff in their journey towards performance enhancement in their own roles. Such work could be seen as similar to that carried out with the players, which could be welcomed by coaching staff, especially where they wish to improve their knowledge of psychological factors in relation to their own performance and that of the players.

54

A difficult yet crucial task that has traditionally been handled in a rather *ad hoc*, and at times unprofessional way, is that of staff recruitment. The game has typically taken people on according to prior knowledge of individuals through word of mouth or testimonies. Although this represents a powerful and at times worthwhile approach to recruitment, the increase in staff numbers and the ever expanding demand for specialists requires a more systematic and rigorous approach to staff recruitment. Sport psychologists may find themselves assisting their colleagues to write, adverts for jobs, new job descriptions and roles and carrying out interviews alongside other members of the backroom staff and coaching team.

This chapter will also deal with matters relating to team building within the staff. Although the sport psychology literature acknowledges the importance of cohesion and sound group dynamics with athletes, little attention has been devoted to creating and sustaining team spirit, cohesion and sound organization amongst staff teams. One of the ways to achieve this is through the use of away days. These typically involve staff physically removing themselves from the environment of the club or training ground in order to 'stand back' and reflect on immediate concerns and practices and to discuss long-term matters. Away days facilitated by the sport psychologist within a Premiership or professional football club can provide an opportunity for staff to think creatively, share ideas across departments and roles and become more aware of the particular demands faced by other colleagues.

Crucially, if managed correctly, these days can help generate camaraderie and team spirit. A more informal and in some ways more conventional psychological approach to developing a cohesive staff team could also involve social gatherings. Sport psychologists may find themselves expected to initiate and organize such occasions. They could also have an opportunity to arrange visits to the theatre, to watch films or attend musical productions and other events that are useful in refreshing the staff and encouraging new insights.

ENCOURAGING 'BUY IN' FROM COACHES AND STAFF

The role of the sport psychologist as an organizational psychologist can only be carried out in an effective and credible way with the support of key staff. It is absolutely essential that the manager, head of sport science and sport medicine, and the academy director are fully committed to supporting the sport psychologist in this role. In order to achieve success, it is necessary for these activities to be carried out throughout the season. This means that there needs to be a clear recognition that these tasks must be delivered during the good periods *and* the difficult moments that a team often faces across the playing season. In some ways, it can be argued that many of these tasks are indeed more vital and essential to assist the performance of coaches and other staff (and, therefore, to the performance of the players) during the most stressful and difficult moments.

Coaches and other staff in Premiership clubs fully understand the importance of performing consistently in their own roles and functions over the season. Managers and coaches are normally acutely aware that training must continue according to plan, irrespective of results in matches. This principle of continuity and consistency is also absolutely essential to the successful implementation of this kind of work delivered by the sport psychologist.

Sport psychologists who find themselves engaged in these types of tasks can often feel that their work is lacking in immediacy. It is sometimes difficult to reconcile this more process-focused role with the need to be seen to be directly affecting the performance of players. However, there is a increasing recognition from the staff and coaches that many of the more mundane, administrative and organizational tasks are an important component in preparing the players before they 'cross the white line'. It has always been acknowledged within professional football that, ultimately, the players determine whether the outcome will be success or failure. Nevertheless, there is a much greater appreciation of the important role that can be played by staff supporting players individually and collectively, so that they arrive at match day in the best possible physical, technical and psychological condition. This should help the organizational psychologist/human resource manager aspect of the sport psychologist's role to become more accepted and received positively at the club.

JOB DESCRIPTIONS

An important task that the sport psychologist can address is to ensure that staff have up-to-date and accurate job descriptions. Within Premiership football and other high-level sport environments, it is essential that staff are fully aware of their responsibilities and understand the duties of their colleagues. In professional football, it is quite rare for coaches and other staff at the training ground to have detailed job descriptions that fully identify the essential and desirable activities they must undertake in their roles. Sport psychologists can use this as an opportunity to make contact with staff at the training ground early in their appointment at a club.

Once again, the support of the manager and other senior staff, including the chairman or chief executive of the club, enhances this process considerably. Job descriptions, recorded in writing after in-depth discussions with individual staff, can help to empower the post holders. Within this type of environment, it is expected that staff will be highly motivated towards their job and committed to the team. What may be less apparent is that for some members of the backroom staff there is often a desire for clarity about the limits of their own role and what is expected of them within this role. Most usually, the culture within a Premiership club tends to informality in relation to this particular issue. It is assumed that staff will know their specific roles and will be sufficiently self-motivated to carry these out to a high standard. In practice, however, there a number of factors that make this a rather simplistic view.

The range of specialist backroom staff at a typical Premiership club, and the increasing complexity brought about by the introduction of more multidisciplinary approaches to player support, has resulted in a more complicated environment. This situation has, by and large, led to many positive new developments. With this, though, has come a greater potential for communication problems and duplication of roles.

Work on clarifying job descriptions can be used to overcome some of the drawbacks associated with having larger staff groups.

Sport psychologists should be able to use individual discussions with staff and coaches about their job descriptions as a way to introduce their own work as a sport psychologist in the club. The process of devising job descriptions enables the sport psychologist to discuss training and development needs of individuals and to prepare staff for appraisals which may be carried out with the manager and assistant manager at mid-point or season end. It is important to note that the aim is not to produce job descriptions that can be used to guide discussions about salary and related matters. Within professional football and in the Premiership it is usual for these matters to be dealt with in other ways, based on perceived market value and the experience of the job holder.

Comprehensive and accurate job descriptions can help the manager, chief executive and other senior management to attain a better understanding of the types of tasks performed in particular posts. This should allow for a clearer evaluation of the importance of this work to the club and make it easier to assess and evaluate achievements of the post holder.

The effectiveness of coaches and other backroom staff can often be enhanced through this process. It also becomes possible to adopt a more professional approach which allows the manager, or a head of department, to select staff against specific job-based criteria. The general lack of formal and agreed job descriptions within the football end of a typical club appears to be an antiquated approach to the managing and guiding of staff.

However, as discussed in Chapter 1, professional football has emerged from a different culture and set of practices to those found in most other commercial or public sector organizations. In most clubs the recruitment of coaches and other support staff, and the identification of specialist roles in areas like sport science and performance analysis, have often evolved in a haphazard and unpredictable fashion. The culture of Premiership football ensures that, given the intense competition between clubs, there is little sharing of good practice. There is also a tendency for knowledge about jobs and roles to be kept informally by the individuals rather than being recorded in written form and in formal

58

documentation. Although this approach has certain advantages, such as ensuring that bureaucracy and managerialism are kept at bay, such *ad hoc* and loose arrangements often means that there is little in-depth or accurate understanding between staff of each others' roles and professional responsibilities.

This in itself can lead to problems. For example, failure to appreciate the full nature of someone's job may lead to conflict and result in staff undermining one another's work. This could cause them to denigrate their colleague's role and work within the club. This behaviour could have an adverse affect on their professional relationship. More important, this could spill out and adversely affect the view that players might have about the value of different roles within the club and the individuals who perform them.

Finally, job descriptions assist the manager and chief executive to identify the areas where they need additional staff or more expertise. Producing an organization chart becomes a more valid and achievable exercise where staff have formally agreed job descriptions. This can assist the club with recruitment policies, promotion and reallocation of work loads and functions where necessary. Given the turbulent financial environment within Premiership football, the organization could benefit from the ability to adjust rapidly and in the right way to maximize use of their resources. It is common to hear in business environments that the staff are the most valuable resource in the organization. There seems to be the same recognition of this within successful and well-run Premiership football clubs.

However, this does not always mean that clubs are run on sound business lines and employ the best management practices when it comes to their staff. Some of this is due to the lack of understanding of some individuals who will have had little exposure to environments other than professional football. For some of these coaches and support staff, job descriptions may initially be viewed with scepticism and considered to be rather unnecessary. Despite this, the sport psychologist can be viewed positively where they take on the role of writing detailed job descriptions. This is sometimes necessary because of the weak writing skills of some staff and a lack of sufficient time to devote to the task. Where the sport psychologist has listened attentively to the member of staff describing their job in a detailed and comprehensive way (maybe also for the first time), there will usually be positive feedback about the process. For some coaches and support staff this task can aid motivation, provide increased focus and bring a sense of pride in the amount of work they carry out and tasks they are responsible for.

Sport psychologists who are unfamiliar with this type of work may wonder if they have the capability to complete this task satisfactorily. Although they might not have had any previous experience of this kind of work and lack certain skills, they will find that their psychological knowledge and understanding of the demands facing staff in professional football mean that they are better placed to perform this job well than either human resource managers or organizational psychologists.

CPD

One of the other activities that the sport psychologist may decide to provide could be to identify a more planned approach to CPD for staff. Job descriptions and structured appraisals can help to identify the training and development needs of individuals and departments. Although some of these will relate to specific professional qualifications, such as those associated with chartered physiotherapy, accredited sport scientists, and chartered sport psychologist, others can be more individually determined and even unique. The sport psychologist may be able to provide training and educational sessions for the coaches and support staff at the club in areas such as stress and anxiety, clinical psychology and referral procedures, psychological factors in working with young players and motivational orientations.

The sport psychologist could take the lead in organizing interdisciplinary training and staff development sessions, where the focus may be on considering a case approach to injured players. This could involve coaches, physiotherapists and sport scientists. The level of knowledge and experience within the staff at a Premiership club may be such that 'in-house' CPD events could be much more in-depth, cutting-edge and applied than their equivalent offered by organizations operating outside this intense environment. For example, a two-hour workshop could be set up to look closely at mechanisms relating to releasing young

60

professional players who fail to make it to the first team. Although there has been some excellent literature on this in recent years (e.g. Gilbourne and Richardson 2005; Pain and Harwood 2007), much of the best contextual knowledge is based in the clubs, especially with the coaching staff, managers, academy directors, heads of education and welfare and others directly involved with young players. Given this situation, it is quite likely that a more detailed account will be delivered by staff at the club than at sessions organized by the FA, universities or other similar organizations.

There is an excellent opportunity to invite world-class speakers and leading figures in a range of football-related, sport or business and education environments, to discuss their own understanding of particular topics and challenges. The additional knowledge and skills that may accrue from such experiences could prove extremely valuable to the staff and the club as a whole. This could be on specific subjects such as dealing with negative media coverage, performance-enhancing drugs in sport, addiction to alcohol and addictive behaviours, or dealing with dislocated expectations (i.e. where the unexpected is the expected!). More general talks might address how to create a team vision, the value of loyalty in staff or how to encourage innovation.

Finally, these types of activities provide a forum to draw staff together to allow for a considered reflection on important matters that they may be wrestling with. These could relate to the club's current situation or be about future challenges. Staff attending talks by esteemed guest speakers at the club could benefit in terms of enhanced confidence in their work, especially when experts in their own speciality, or in other fields, are able to confirm the high standards and excellence of their existing practices in the club. CPD sessions of this type that take place on a frequent and regular basis over the season can also assist with staff motivation and morale. This can become particularly important during those difficult moments that will inevitably occur in such a high pressured and stressful environment.

Workshops, seminars and talks delivered in an informal and open style that suits the culture of professional football can also provide a forum where confidential dialogue can take place between colleagues, in a supportive and constructive way. Again, this is extremely important for sport psychologists to facilitate because of the difficulties in this environment of bringing groups of the staff together when there are so many competing demands and when their work is subject to significant pressures arising from lack of time and resources.

It is the sport psychologist's job to make sure that these moments are carefully planned opportunities for the staff and coaches to come together for specific issues, and that they help increase the quantity and quality of interpersonal communication in the club.

CODES OF CONDUCT

Another way that the sport psychologist can assist practices and policy is through a code of conduct. This could be applicable to all players and can be constructed with their input. In terms of the staff, a code of conduct can be agreed upon to allow staff to more formally record best working practices and expectations concerning their roles and behaviour.

Although players usually have a legally enforceable code that is included within their employment contract, this does not preclude the possibility of devising a document addressing broader concerns. For example, the players' code of conduct can deal with identifying what is acceptable behaviour for players on the training ground, on match days and in their public lives. This last point is important given the high profile and extensive media interest in players' personal lives and off-field activities.

The sport psychologist can use this exercise to generate feedback from players and staff about what they think constitutes desirable profes-sional behaviour, and how this should be enforced. The code of conduct can help players to reflect on their responsibilities beyond performing and winning matches and extend to identifying the ethos they would like to help generate at the club.

The specific areas that could be covered include a system for player fines, penalties for poor timekeeping, and arrangements concern-ing external appointments and limits on socializing. As elite-level professional athletes who have to perform at ever increasing levels, information about diet, nutrition and alcohol consumption could also be useful to include.

It may also be important to consider how players should behave on match days in terms of acceptance about team selection, behaviour on being substituted, and responses to bookings or being sent off. Some of the instructions may be detailed and precise, and because of this they could be easy to monitor. In contrast, other statements may be intended to help players to acknowledge their broader responsibilities to other members of the team, staff or the wider public.

Some of the specific statements that could be contained within a code of conduct may be aimed at identifying rules and procedures that can contribute to a positive attitude amongst the team. For example, in attempting to create a culture of excellence some of the following statements relating to standards of behaviour might assist the process of inculcating a good ethos amongst players:

- Players should endeavour to respect each others' views and opinions.
- It is important for players to be honest with themselves and in dealings with others around them in an effort to create trust and commitment to their goals.
- There should be an attempt to keep disruptive and negative issues relating to football 'in-house' so as not to cause unnecessary distraction and negativity.
- A professional approach should be adopted in all activities; this professional identity must be maintained within the club and when in public at all times.
- Players are expected to offer constructive critical feedback at the right times to each other and the staff. It is essential that this is done in order to find a resolution to a problem and move the team forward.
- It is important for players to acknowledge that the staff are there to support and guide them where possible, and that they are equally motivated to do the best for each individual player and the team.

The code of conduct can also be a 'living' document in that with new situations and changes in playing staff, goals, standards or coaching staff there may be a need to adjust requirements in order that success can be further developed. The sport psychologist will have an opportunity to look in detail at what changes need to be made to the code of conduct from time to time. This is a two-way process. In the first instance it may be beneficial and motivational to ask all players, only senior players, or groups representing the squad to give feedback on changes that they feel are necessary. For example, some clubs are reluctant to identify and share weekly schedules with players.

Whilst there are many sound reasons behind this traditional practice, it could be that players are confused and even demotivated at times by being unable to access this information. This could be particularly true with players who have joined the Premier League or a professional football club from other countries and cultures where practices relating to sharing information could be considerably different. It may also cause problems where players have significant family responsibilities, or if they are new to the club, and therefore have important domestic and personal matters to sort out.

It is also possible for the playing staff to suggest the types of behaviours, policies or practices that they would like to see applied in the club as a whole. In other words, this can be an opportunity to identify attitudes, behaviours and methods of communication that will apply equally to playing and coaching staff. Although this may be a difficult task for the sport psychologist to achieve, it can be an excellent way to assess the level of cohesion that exists throughout the team and the club as a whole.

The staff may have their own largely informal and unwritten code of conduct that they generally acknowledge and work within. Although it may present an arduous challenge for the sport psychologist, a formally agreed and written staff code of conduct could be a useful document for a number of reasons. Similar to the situation pertaining to players, the exercise to agree upon and record a code of conduct can be an excellent vehicle to generate dialogue between staff about their expectations and standards of practice. It is also a means of demonstrating that the staff are prepared to abide by agreed standards in much the same way as the players.

Finally, it is important to point out that a code of conduct is much more than a list of rules. Although it is true that players (or the staff and coaches) will not spend a great deal of time regularly studying and scrutinizing this document, it is nevertheless another way of helping to create a professional, unified and high performance culture within the club.

AWAY DAY RATIONALE

The sport psychologist can also be involved in a number of activities that can assist the staff to guide their work in the longer term. One of the difficulties in a performance environment where results can change mood, perceptions and behaviours in such a short space of time is that longer-term goals can be ignored or forgotten.

It is of vital importance that the players and staff are aware of the vision of the club as a whole. Statements about vision may be in the form of aims and objectives, or words addressing philosophy of practice or long-term goals. The way this is done or expressed is much less important than the fact that, especially for the staff, there is a series of agreed statements pointing to the future. Without these, energy may be completely devoted to the next match and that alone.

Although it is a generally accepted cliché in performance sport that focus should be on the next game, this does not mean that longer-term goals and plans are not kept in mind. Maintaining a long-term view is absolutely essential to ensure that players and staff do not 'overinvest' in a match that ultimately may not deliver the desired performance or result. The sport psychologist is able to draw on examples from successful and leading world business organizations, as well as many top-level sport teams who are able to provide evidence of the importance of maintaining a clear vision for the future during good and difficult periods.

To assist staff and coaches to keep their focus on future development needs and the medium-term issues the sport psychologist may find that the staff will benefit from being able to take part in away days. These events should be organized to occur away from the training ground or the stadium and provide an ideal opportunity for staff to speak openly and freely about important issues that they are facing beyond day to day operational matters.

The use of this kind of staff development event is familiar to commercial and public sector organizations but may be considered novel in elite football and professional team sport. The sport psychologist can shape the agenda in such a way that these events can address a number of different concerns. The day can be structured to ensure that in-depth dialogue takes place across departments and between individuals. Within the normal working day it is often difficult to find sufficient time to engage in detailed and sometimes complex discussions on important topics; this is especially the case where these are not urgent or must be addressed immediately. The day can be used to assist staff to understand the role and functions of other colleagues and their activities more fully. This can lead to the development of better cooperation and greater multidisciplinary and interdisciplinary working between the staff.

AWAY DAY ACTIVITIES

The following section describes some of the activities that could be included in a typical agenda for an away day.

Kicking the day off

The day could commence with an opportunity for all staff to ask questions, either anonymously, or to the group, in relation to any matter that they feel is important to the success of the team and their role in the club. This can be a cathartic experience for some. It can also provide an opportunity for senior staff and coaches to raise topics in a non-confrontational and constructive way, and allow individuals to demonstrate their commitment to and knowledge of their role. This final point is extremely important given that the culture of Premiership and professional football tends to be action-oriented, fast-paced and unreflective.

For some staff this experience of putting forward their views to the group can be daunting. The sport psychologist should ensure that the atmosphere at away days is businesslike yet informal. This will help all staff to participate fully, and be an ideal occasion to allow new or less experienced staff to offer their views without fear or favour. The day can also be enjoyable from a social point of view, especially where activities are built in around team-building exercises, and a more relaxed social occasion can be provided after the formal part of the day is concluded.

The following represent some of the kinds of issues and subjects that could profitably be discussed at an away day or similar type of event in a professional football club:

Reviewing performance during phases of the season

This can involve exercises based on studying data that captures team and individual player performances over the season or a part of the season. A review of goal-setting, for example, could identify which targets have been met and make adjustments for the stages to come. Analysis here could focus on physical statistics from training, match performance data, injury figures and any other quantifiable information that can assist current assessments and future planning.

Coaches and the staff could also spend time clarifying what they consider to be departmental non-negotiables; these are tasks and responsibilities that must be carried out without exception. This exercise can help staff to identify and discuss their own roles and responsibilities, how these relate to those of their department and how they assist the work of other staff and the whole team. It can help maintain focus, prevent duplication of effort and improve synergy. An open and detailed discussion like this can additionally help to make interdisciplinary work more desirable and feasible.

Periodization

Especially at the start of a season, or, even better, during the pre-season phase, it can be useful to identify key activities, targets and goals that each department needs to achieve over the year. This exercise allows for work to be managed in a planned and systematic way. It is also of vital importance in ensuring that adequate rest and recovery periods are identified in advance.

The document that emerges from this task can be amended and adjusted as the season progresses and as needs change. It may be difficult to produce a detailed plan for the whole season because of the large number of factors that impinge on the day-to-day, weekly and monthly activities at a Premier League football club. Nevertheless, this exercise has great psychological value in that it can assist coaches and the staff to feel more in control of their work and to be able to anticipate potential problems in a planned and systematic way. Further, it can generate increased feelings of confidence due to staff being able to identify specific and important duties that will be delivered.

Data analysis, trends and benchmarking

The increasing use of video-based player performance measuring systems like Prozone and Amisco has meant that there is a plethora of match-based data for professional football clubs to interpret in their preparation for individual games, phases of the season or for the whole competitive cycle. Performance analysis staff at the club can have an important role to play in helping coaches and other colleagues make best use of the data available from these systems. An away day can provide an ideal opportunity for staff to examine the data closely and interrogate the findings that emerge. The performance analysts, with the support of the sport psychologist, could lead a review of the team's physical, technical, tactical and psychological data in order to identify trends and predict possible patterns. Subsequent analysis of this by the staff in small working groups will ensure that a multidisciplinary lens is applied, and that the requirements of a particular discipline taken in isolation will not excessively influence future plans.

This presents an opportunity to reflect on the standards that players have achieved and can help staff to redirect focus at particular areas in order to meet the required levels. This data can be compared in a benchmarking exercise against other similar clubs in the league in order to assess current and projected levels of performance.

It may be desirable to look at each player's needs in turn, and devise a work programme for the next phase of the season to address individual needs. This can be achieved through input from the coaches, sport

68

science staff, scouting, and medical staff, to ensure that a multidisciplinary perspective is used in this process.

Academy matters

Away days provide an opportunity to assess the development of young players in the squad, and in Premier League teams, to look more carefully at the function of the academy. This is an opportunity for first team staff to understand the needs and difficulties facing those charged with the development of young players at the club.

This is important on a number of levels. First, the progress of young players into first team football is crucial for everyone at the club. The investment in the development of young talented players makes it even more vital that clubs manage this process carefully and skilfully. The focus on first team results and performances, although fully understandable, can mean that much less attention is devoted to the development of young players. An away day can be the platform for broader discussions about how the first team staff and broader processes can assist the work of the academy. A further benefit is that this dialogue might contribute to an exchange of ideas between staff, that may enhance the practices of coaches and others working with young players.

Presentations by external speakers

Individuals from high-achieving cultures, whether in education, business or sporting environments can be inspirational if used appropriately at an away day event. The speaker can be selected on the basis of their knowledge of a particular challenge or issue that the club are currently facing. For example, an individual who has successfully managed a large business organization during difficult economic and financial circumstances could have a crucial message that first team staff can draw upon and relate to their own situation. The profile of elite professional sports clubs and Premiership football means that it is relatively easy to attract a wide range of impressive speakers. These individuals are often curious to find out more about elite sport environments and how they manage themselves in such a purely performance-focused culture.

The experience of listening to such individuals can also bring a great sense of perspective for staff at the club, especially when the speaker is talking about work or activities that involve matters to do with health and people's livelihoods. Hearing about the similarities between creating standards of excellence and optimal performance in a disparate range of cultures and organizations can be particularly powerful in reassuring staff abut their existing practices. Some of the stories from these elite level sports organizations have been documented by Gilson *et al.* (2001) in their impressive series of studies across a wide range of teams operating at the highest of levels of professional sport.

AWAY DAY CULTURE CHANGE

An away day or other similar event can allow the sport psychologist to develop a stronger team identity and improve group cohesion through staff working together as equals. The relative informality and avoidance of hierarchy will often help to put the staff in a relaxed mood and positive mindset. The sport psychologist may be able to deliver educational sessions on key psychological factors like stress, anxiety and goal-setting, but in such a way that staff are positive about this input since it sits naturally alongside other developmental tasks on the agenda.

The concept of an away day can be varied significantly to reflect levels of staff understanding and their particular needs at any given point in the season. This means that the types of activities must reflect the needs of both the staff and the club at its current stage of development, but they must encourage individuals to look beyond immediate concerns to consider the future and what must be done to increase the likelihood of success.

Within a Premiership football club there will be many individuals whose entire working life has been within the environment of professional football. Although many in business and education settings are familiar with the notion of staff training and development days, to many football coaches and staff away days and team-building exercises might

70

be quite an alien concept. This can mean that the sport psychologist must take great care to ensure that staff approach the day in a positive and a constructive way. To assist this, the sport psychologist could decide to carry out individual meetings prior to the day to explain the philosophy and intended outcomes of the event.

The away day agenda also represents a powerful opportunity for the sport psychologist to build bridges with staff, especially those who may be sceptical about the need for such an event. This scepticism may stem from a lack of understanding about the value of away days. It may also reflect a perception that the day will focus mainly on psychological development rather than on matters of real substance, most of which will not be to do with psychology specifically, and most crucially, that it will take away valuable time from important daily activities. The sport psychologist must be careful to ensure that away days are opportunities for genuine participation from all members of staff. However, the reality is that as a result of personality differences, confidence, anxiety related to the tasks and concern about sharing ideas with other staff in more senior positions (such as the manager), there may be a slower rate of acceptance of the value of away days from some individuals.

The agenda should ideally be constructed alongside the staff; agenda items should reflect their concerns and needs rather than those of the sport psychologist. This also ensures for greater participation, especially where sessions are led by departments or individual members of staff.

A powerful aid to ensuring that the discussions on the day are actually carried out afterwards is to record them and make written accounts available to all staff after the event. This summary of key points emerging from the day can be used to remind staff of agreements that were made, action points to be addressed and tasks to be completed before the next away day. Although some individuals will choose not to read this written record of the day, for others this is a powerful record of the individual and collective thought processes at different points of the season. The sport psychologist may feel that between six and eight full formal away days over the season are necessary to bring the greatest benefits possible. These may be supplemented with more irregular and frequently occurring meetings every four to six weeks to address more immediate concerns that must be dealt with in the shorter term.

Finally, without the support from the manager and preferably two or three other key staff at the club, the sport psychologist will have great difficulty in providing a series of effective and inspirational away days. Where a manager and their key staff understands and values this developmental activity, away days can represent a remarkable opportunity and an important occasion to strengthen the staff team, sustain morale and enhance practices. If this is true during the most successful times at a club, it is arguably even more true when a club, that is the staff *and* players, are being assailed in the media for poor results, and when they are at the lower end of the league or in the relegation zone.

4

SUPPORTING THE MANAGER

Sport psychologists may have an ideal opportunity to support the manager in their work and to increase the knowledge of this individual about the use of sport psychology to enhance the performance of the team and the staff. The manager or head coach of a high-level or professional sport organization is someone who may often find they have to make difficult decisions alone. Although this can be an attractive and enjoyable aspect of the role, it does place considerable demands upon the individual concerned. Undoubtedly, some of these challenges are centred on the level of managerial expertise and technical knowledge that the individual possesses. Other demands relate to the need to be a leader who is as adept at operating effectively on the ground with coaches and players as at higher levels within the organization, with chief executives, directors and owners.

The sport psychologist may be able to establish a series of regular and frequent individual meetings with the manager or head coach where the aim is to provide psychological support for them to maximize their performance in the job and to develop their knowledge of the importance of psychological factors in high-performance environments. The sport psychologist may be able to help the manager through discussions about dealing with their own professional and personal goals and ambitions. They may also be useful in terms of suggesting how to deal with anxiety and stress, and maintaining focus. The psychologist can further help the manager in the area of leadership and associated skills and qualities. Finally, the process of working with the psychologist may help develop the level of self-awareness, and ultimately, the self-knowledge of the manager. This relates in turn to managers' identity and the deeper levels of meaning they attach to important events in their lives. This apparently philosophical dimension may turn out to be the most important skill they can acquire, especially to assist them to deal successfully with the volatility inherent in the job.

Arguably, some of these skills and new forms of knowledge can be developed through use of formal appraisal systems carried out by senior staff in the club. This may involve owners, the chief executive or chairman and human resource managers. However, the sport psychologist, through a series of in-depth confidential one-to-one meetings, may be able to address all these factors outside and beyond any formal processes. This can have great value since the focus is strictly on development and not tied to formal mechanisms such as performance appraisals.

The following account attempts to capture the dialogue that can take place between the sport psychologist and manager or head coach when they are meeting to focus on the development of the manager themselves.

DEVELOPING THE MANAGER

Within such a high-profile and public role there is considerable need for managers of a professional football club to develop the capacity to examine themselves, reflect on their decisions and acquire skills and personal qualities that will help them achieve more. It is an often repeated assertion that being at 'the top' can be a lonely place. This statement is made for a number of reasons, such as how people view their leaders or those at the highest point in the hierarchy, the difficulty of sharing confidential information and the fact that many others await in the wings, ready to replace the manager should they fall. All these factors can bring considerable stress and anxiety and make it difficult for individuals to consult with others about their plans and to garner accurate views about how they are perceived externally.

This semi-fictitious vignette attempts to capture the type of dialogue that could take place between the sport psychologist and a manager in this situation.

74

The sport psychologist arrived at the agreed venue some twenty minutes before the manager. He always tried to do this to ensure he could prepare any additional plans in line with media reports or general developments that had taken place the previous evening. This was also an opportunity to compose himself and read over previous notes to remind him of the important themes that they had recently addressed and the action points still to be pursued. Depending on the manager, it could be best to conduct the meeting in a highly informal style, where little if any recording of notes takes place within the session. However, after the meeting there may be an ideal opportunity to put this material down in writing which will provide useful records for future sessions, and may allow interim reports to be prepared for the manager to read at a later date.

The sport psychologist should always pay considerable attention to choosing a location for the meeting that allows for privacy and conveys a professional approach to their work. However, great care should also be taken to select a venue that will provide an inspirational backdrop to the meeting. For example, this could be somewhere that is personally significant to the manager's career and recent past, or could be where spectacular views or beautiful scenery can be seen easily during the meeting. It is of vital importance that the environment is conducive to a business like approach but which nevertheless is different to a usual workplace setting, and is somewhere that can evoke positive and powerful emotions.

As the manager sat down they placed their phones on the table and apologized that they would have to take two calls if these came through during the meeting. For some sport psychologists this may seem impossible to reconcile with the need for an in-depth and detailed session. However, depending on the demands faced by the manager, their personality, leadership style and mood, it may be that the sport psychologist has to accept a less than ideal situation if he is going to be able to conduct meetings successfully in this culture.

'How do you think you are handling what's been happening in the past four weeks, and have you ever been in something quite like this before in your career?' asked the sport psychologist.

'Well, I have but I don't think I handled it particularly well if I'm honest,' said the manager. He continued with his reflections about why he had not been able to deal in the past with a similar challenge to the one that he now faced. 'Maybe I spent too much time focusing on individual players and their problems,' he continued. 'I think that this was how I had been successful in the past. The game is ultimately about one group of players against another group. Maybe this can be forgotten at times.'

The sport psychologist listened intently to this analysis and asked the manager whether they felt that they were able to turn things around on their own, or if they needed more support from other staff members, or people beyond the group. 'Are you sure that you made the right decisions or assessed things accurately when you last faced similar difficulties to those you now face, or was it because you yourself were not convinced about the path that you took?'

This type of question has been discussed within the sport psychology literature in terms of stress and coping (Nicholls 2007). Drawing on a cognitive behavioural approach, a distinction has been made between problem-focused and emotion-focused strategies for coping with stress. Although these constructs can be useful for researchers when attempting to categorize particular thoughts and behaviours, this is much less viable when carrying out applied work in a one-to-one setting. An existential phenomenological psychology perspective would argue that if such a thing as a coping strategy or technique exists, it is always constituted of a mix of emotion- and problem-focused aspects. This does not mean that it is impossible to talk about each separately, however, as this dialogue reveals, in reality (i.e. empirically speaking) there is no such thing as a purely problem-focused or emotion-focused strategy. For example, if the so-called emotion-focused technique requires the individual to maintain their level of self-belief then this cannot be achieved through thoughts and feelings alone.

To be effective the thoughts and feelings must relate to existing and future behaviour and an effort must be made to improve on all of these aspects simultaneously. Without this, it is illogical to claim that good and positive emotions are beneficial. The test of their effectiveness can only be in terms of their impact on thoughts and behaviours. This is consistent with an holistic approach and is associated with humanistic, gestalt, existential and other-person-centred approaches in counselling psychology.

'What exactly did you do well last time in this situation, and what is so different now?' asked the sport psychologist.

'I expect more from myself this time round,' said the manager. 'My expectations about myself have changed. I am not satisfied to hope for the best; I need to know that what I am doing is the best, and is "going to work".'

'Is that something you have seen or experienced before as a player, or earlier in your management career? If it is, what was that like and how did that make you feel?' the sport psychologist asked.

'It's never been that clear,' said the manager. 'Sometimes I feel that something is right, but don't really know whether it really is, or not. I don't think that given my experience, I should still feel this way in these tough moments. I know what I am expected to do at this phase, but I wonder if there is something else I should do, and the biggest thing is for the first time in a long time I am doubting myself and my decisions more than normal. I have had this experience before but usually when I have been a bloody idiot, by putting myself forward to speak to the media or some group of experts on subjects that I know I don't know, and I know that they know I don't really know!'

At this the manager laughed out loud and looked across the room at a couple who had just sat down to order their food. 'I bet they would not believe the kind of conversation we are having,' started the manager. 'There is so much front needed at times. Do you think that great leaders are mostly front and are able to say anything to anyone, especially what people want to hear at that time?'

As a sport psychologist, I wanted to give a clear answer to this question and to provide a research-informed and theoretically derived explanation of the experience of feeling uncertain about confidence and knowledge, despite being a highly experienced and successful person. It is at moments such as these that a sport psychologist guided by an existential phenomenological approach is reminded that uncomfortable dialogue should sometimes be allowed to run its course, and that the best solutions are those where the client struggles with themselves to construct an answer. The task here for the sport psychologist is, sometimes gently and at other times with more surety, to guide the dialogue towards an authentic, ethically sound and achievable solution.

After a further fifteen minutes discussing the details of the current crisis facing the club and the team, the sport psychologist began to draw the session to some type of conclusion.

'So, what are your options to move on through this real challenge? Is this going to be a moment when you learn something huge and important about yourself, your skills, personality and values? Will you emerge out of the other side a better leader and as someone even more confident about being able to achieve your goals and ambition as a manager in the game?'

At these words the manager stared through the windows. The rain was slowly beginning to drift in over the hills.

'It would be really good to get away from this depressing and dull weather just so people can lift their heads up off the floor, don't you think,' asked the manager. 'I sometimes think that we are like the weather, that when its nice, clear and sunny everything seems perfect, but it's not though, not really, and when we have rubbish weather, it makes you think everything is doom and gloom, and all is lost! That's not true either though, is it, that's just for those people who have given up the fight and now follow their emotions and feelings and don't believe they can make a difference.'

At this comment, the sport psychologist knew that they had been right not to have talked about adopting a problem-focused or emotion-focused coping strategy, and that the account just provided by the manager represented reality much more closely than any hypothetical psychological constructs could ever have. However, the sport psychologist was aware that the loose ends and the barrier in the encounter about the issue of whether feeling fully in control or sufficiently competent to deal with some challenges had been resolved in some way.

'What makes you step forward to make decisions even when you are unsure if they are the correct ones or likely to be helpful?' asked the sport psychologist.

The manager was busy packing up their papers into their briefcase and having a last gulp of tea. He looked directly at the sport psychologist and said, 'What other choice do I have!? If I don't make a decision then I am not doing my job, and I may as well give it all up. Just because it is not clear what will happen, I know that I can't avoid doing what I am going to do. If people want to see this negatively, or if some think I am trying to help them specially then I can't do anything about that perception. But it is important that I know I am not making decisions for the benefit or not of particular individuals, whether I like them personally or not, what I am absolutely convinced of is that I must take action that I believe to be the best for the team and the club in the whole. Just because I am not one hundred per cent comfortable about what I am going to do, does not mean that I do not believe it is the right and most appropriate action to take!'

By now the manager was on his feet, and as he strode purposely out of the room his mobile phone rang. I overheard him saying that he was going to pull the staff together for a meeting later that day and that he wanted to put something important to us all. I sat for a minute, collecting my own thoughts and quickly completing some brief notes relating to the meeting that had just taken place.

The manager had not been involved in a twenty-five-minute meeting where the result had been new set of goals, or a detailed plan of action to be followed systematically. Although these are clearly needed at times, the aim of this session had been more truly psychological and personal. At its heart was the dilemma facing everyone, especially those facing challenging situations or critical moments. According to an existential psychology interpretation, the manager was involved in the need to acknowledge that choices must often be made without full knowledge about their likely outcomes, and that the anxiety surrounding these is a natural and inevitable accompaniment. In order to help them to successfully confront this anxiety the manager met with the sport psychologist. It is this type of anxiety that has been written about in a profound and deep way by writers such as Kierkegaard (1944 [1844]). His work provides a complex, elegant and grounded description and analysis of the anxiety of choice and decision.

When high achievers, leaders and eminent individuals speak about the loneliness at the top, they echo much of what Kierkegaard and other existential psychologists have had to say on the matter over the past 150 years. One of the most significant demands placed upon a person in a position of leadership and responsibility is that, ultimately, they will have to take momentous decisions with or without the support of others, and that it is often impossible to be fully open with those who will be affected by these choices. For a manager in such a high-profile sport as professional football these decisions will require them to search deeply into themselves, their past experiences and beliefs to help them to identify a way forward.

The sport psychologist can provide a modest but important role when a manager faces these moments at critical stages in the development of a team, or a group of individuals. The sport psychologist is able to offer a completely confidential, psychologically informed and contextually knowledgeable encounter that may assist the manager to accept his responsibility to choose, and to choose wisely with new consideration given to achieving immediate or long-term goals, and doing this in an ethical and professional way.

PROFESSIONAL AND PERSONAL GOALS AND AMBITIONS

Another important function that the sport psychologist can provide in his work with the manager is to help with career planning and ambitions for the future.

Although there are many key individuals who can be involved in this work, the sport psychologist possesses particular skills and knowledge that can provide something quite different. These others, for example, could include the manager's agent, the chief executive, directors or club owners. It may also be the case that useful advice and guidance can be provided by mentors from non-sport backgrounds with experience of working with high-achieving individuals in business, media and the entertainment industry. There are certain topics, however, that would be difficult to discuss with most, if not all of these individuals. For example, the manager may be unable to speak with his current employers about a desire to move eventually to a larger club, work abroad or develop other skills such as a learning a foreign language. These and other developmental activities might be interpreted negatively, and could result in the chairman, owners and others questioning the manager's level of commitment to their current position.

The sport psychologist can help the manager to construct a series of goals relating to their long-term career aspirations. This can assist with the identification of a number of short-term, realistic and achievable goals that can be pursued by the manager with or without the support of the club, to help them to achieve their long-term goals.

The sport psychologist can usefully break down the short-term goals into a number of broad areas, each of which could be useful in helping the manager to adopt a more focused approach to their personal and professional development. These can be written down and used by both parties to inform dialogue and decision making.

Alternatively, the manager may be satisfied that the sport psychologist maintains some written accounts of their discussions purely for their own use. Depending on his style and personality, the manager might be more comfortable with a less systematic and formal approach to the recording of meetings and dialogue.

In terms of short-term goals, the sport psychologist could assist the manager to identify that they need to increase their skills and knowledge through pursuing educational opportunities. This could mean that the manager needs to develop a greater understanding about sports science related theory to allow him to acquire an in-depth understanding of how this can assist performance in the sport. The intention would be to improve knowledge that could help him appoint the best staff and to see more clearly how sport science can be used to support and inform the work of the coaching team.

One of the difficulties facing managers in an elite professional sports team setting is their lack of specialist and advanced levels of knowledge about every aspect of their work. This means that they will have to delegate certain elements to other staff. Nevertheless, it is essential that they have sufficient understanding of sport science to recognize its limitations and be confident about the benefits it can bring.

The sport psychologist may have strong links with local universities or have maintained close ties to research centres and professional bodies in sport science and sport psychology. This can allow them to identify opportunities for managers to develop their knowledge further. This could involve arranging bespoke courses, inviting experts and researchers into the club to deliver educational sessions for the manager, and if appropriate, to other key staff.

The sport psychologist, especially where they have studied sport science or a related discipline earlier in their own educational journey, may be in a strong position to help the manager appreciate the benefits of integrating sport science more fully in work with the players. Information and research relating to nutrition, diet, football-specific fitness and the mechanics of movement could be presented informally or in a systematic way to the manager.

Clearly, the sport psychologist has an opportunity to discuss the latest sport psychology research and to expose the manager to new or complex ideas from the discipline. This is likely to be an important role for the sport psychologist given that elite-level coaches are often highly motivated to develop their psychological knowledge to complement their usually advanced level of understanding of the technical, tactical and physical requirements of the sport. Through working with the manager

82

in this way, the sport psychologist will find it easier to explain the value of multidisciplinary or interdisciplinary approaches to the delivery of sport science in a team. The manager within professional football has an important influence on the attitudes of staff towards the place of sports science in football. A manager with an in-depth and subtle appreciation of the value of sport science in professional football will be a much stronger advocate than the sport psychologist when implementing change in practices. This relates to their position in the hierarchy, but also to the fact that in professional football and high-level sport there is a considerable amount of distrust of 'boffins' or 'academics' who are perceived to be strong on theory and research but often lacking in the appropriate level of applied knowledge. It is to be hoped that this obstacle to the integration of sport science can be overcome through having a manager sufficiently educated and aware about what different disciplines can contribute and how important it is to manage the interface between sport science, sport medicine and coaching in such intensely performance-oriented environments.

Managers may wish to study a language to allow them to consider moving abroad in the future, or to enhance their communication skills with overseas players in their team. In addition, learning basic conservational skills could help them in their work with players' agents, international media and relating to players' families and friends. The sport psychologist could arrange for instruction to take place at the club or at home, or by following a more conventional academic programme. Again, the sport psychologist could easily justify carrying out the work involved in setting up these opportunities because if they can support the work of the manager in terms of their professional and personal development this may well have a positive impact on the manager's work overall and impact positively on his effectiveness with players and staff. Although this may appear to be primarily aimed at improving the career opportunities for the manager in the future, the acquisition of skills in another language and the increased understanding of another culture will undoubtedly help in the manager's role with the club.

Other educational experiences that may be worthwhile relate to finance, business strategy, injury prevention and management. For example, the sport psychologist may be able to contact academics, researchers or business consultants in order to help the manager acquire a more advanced understanding of finance, corporate governance and strategy. There is little doubt that many managers and senior coaches pick up a wide-ranging and in-depth appreciation of some of these matters in their dealings concerning player recruitment, staff recruitment and through working to budgets and bidding for resources. Although most do not usually possess high-level formal academic qualifications in account-ancy or strategic planning, managers in elite-level professional sport will find themselves operating alongside other senior individuals at the club who routinely possess such qualifications and experience. There are courses offered through the Professional Footballers' Association (PFA), the Football Association (FA) and universities, through which aspiring and existing managers can be introduced to the techniques and skills of business management and finance. Although admirable, these programmes cannot equip managers in professional football for the myriad of issues that they must deal with or be aware of.

The sport psychologist could set up a series of regular meetings with business consultants and academics who possess high levels of con-textual knowledge in relation to professional sport and professional football in particular. Fortunately, there are a growing number of such individuals and consultancies in operation. Most are based in manage-ment and business studies departments in universities, or exist within highly successful consultancies that operate generally in top end public and private business organizations. In my experience, the manager will benefit greatly from even a relatively brief level of exposure to the ideas of these individuals or organizations. Because they are from outside of the club, it is easier to ensure that managers can speak openly and freely about the areas they would like to understand better, and the topics or skills they would like to know more about to enhance their current role and future careers in the sport.

In addition, the business consultant who is used to working with other organizations in highly pressured, competitive and stressful business environments will have a wealth of examples from outside of football, or other professional sports, that can stimulate the thinking and deepen the manager's understanding.

Although the manager may not aspire to move roles and become a chief executive, chairman or director at the club, his hand can be strengthened by attaining a greater appreciation of the challenges faced by individuals in these roles. This could also assist him in terms of how he should present requests for additional resources to the club directors. It can also be useful to show why there is a need to have synergy between team goals, club aspirations and the financial and strategic direction of the organization as a whole.

Such knowledge does not mean that managers will become an expert in detailed legal issues, accountancy practices or operations management. However, it does mean that their important and frequent dealings with the Board and other senior individuals in the club will be based on a sound and thorough appreciation of the roles, methods and aims that govern the activities of these individuals.

The sport psychologist may also find that their own function (described in Chapter 2 as being more akin to that of an organizational or occupational psychologist), could be better understood as a result of this type of initiative. Through acquiring a more formal and detailed view, the manager may be able to acknowledge the need for someone to help manage processes between departments and individuals in the team to help achieve the long-term aims.

This could prove to be useful in terms of allowing the sport psychologist to take on much of the work that is carried out by performance directors, or directors of football in some clubs. It may be that as a result of this process through which a manager begins to recognize and acknowledge how important it is to understand the strategic activities of the club that he will support the sport psychologist should he or she wish to take a more active role in this work themselves. The sport psychologist alternatively may use this new awareness to stress the need to appoint a performance director or an operations manager who will be able to work specifically at the interface between the club and the team. The appointment of such a person could help the sport psychologist in a number of ways. The most important of these could be that it allows him or her to maintain one-to-one support for the players, and helps to establish a high-performance culture amongst the staff who work directly with the team.

A director of performance would be able to work closely with the sport psychologist on issues relating to the recruitment and development of staff and players, and crucially, would be able to devote a major part of the role to ensuring that where possible, a symbiotic relationship exists between the activities and aspirations of the football club staff (usually located at the stadium) and of the coaching and football staff based at the training ground.

APPRAISAL MECHANISMS

The sport psychologist may be able to carry out a different type of professional and personal appraisal meeting from that carried out by the manager's superior. This confidential series of meetings could be completely directed towards identifying the future aspirations and ambitions of the manager. Inevitably, some of these will relate to matters like acquiring new staff, changing players and trying to engender a different mentality and set of targets for the team and the club. The demands of each of these can be discussed in a number of ways; however, it may be useful to assess their impact from a psychological perspective.

In other words, each goal or target could be examined in terms of what types of psychological demands they place on the manager and whether they currently possess, or possibly need to acquire, the necessary skills and personal qualities to be able to meet these challenges. The sport psychologist may recommend that the manager needs to learn how to control their negative emotions more carefully, or discuss how important it is to accept that there will be large frustrations along the path to these goals. Although not easy to accept and address, these types of specific tasks facing the manager may prove to be decisive in terms of whether or not they will eventually achieve success in their job.

Managers sometimes set themselves more or less unachievable goals, given the resources of their current club. They may expect to achieve a particular level of success in a relatively short time having done so rapidly in the past or at a previous club. The discussion here will not be primarily about ensuring that goals and goal-setting are consistent with the SMARTER requirements outlined by sport psychologists like Gould (2001). Of much greater significance will be how the sport psychologist can assist the manager to recognize patterns emerging from their past

86

successes and analyse whether they have a tendency towards being over-ambitious or lacking in ambition.

The discussion could become a much deeper personal and philosophical dialogue, where managers are required to scrutinize why they are constantly ambitious or more easily satisfied with their achievements within Premiership football. In general, the manager will be expected by a range of stakeholders, such as the media, the fans and the board of directors, to display a high level of confidence in their ability to reach their goals. The culture of Premier League football arguably makes it more likely that managers will be prepared to publicly express highly ambitious targets for themselves personally and for their team, no matter how difficult their current plight. A manager who is realistic, and has identified goals for himself and the team that would satisfy much sport psychology research and theory on this topic over the last thirty years (e.g. Duda *et al.* 1995), could soon find himself out of a job because of a perceived lack of self-belief and ambition.

However, within such a culture, the sport psychologist could use confidential meetings with the manager to raise their awareness of the serious implications of appearing to be too ambitious or encouraging unrealistic expectations. It is extremely important that managers maintain a sense of reality. This means that, although they may feel obliged, and even be pressured into making ambitious claims for themselves, the team or the club, it is crucial that they know what really can be achieved next, and what they can reasonably be expected to strive for as they progress in their career.

HUMILITY

When a team has a good run of results it will invariably attract a huge amount of positive coverage. This will be captured locally, internationally, and, given the status of the Premier League, sometimes even on a global scale. Although this can assist motivation and psychological momentum (Crust 2007), it is important that the manager (and the players, staff and sport psychologist) do not 'believe their own press'. There is nothing more certain in sport that a good run of results will end sooner or later, and that a difficult phase of defeats, or at least a prolonged period of indifferent form, will immediately follow.

The sport psychologist needs to ensure that the manager maintains the key psychological quality and philosophical virtue of humility, especially in those most dangerous of moments where success and achievement seem effortless and unlikely to end. The experienced manager will already know from being in the sport for many years as a player and coach that failure and some level of humiliation is usually just around the corner. This does not mean that the sport psychologist needs to remind the manager of this fact, or convince him to dampen the mood amongst players and staff in preparation for the inevitable moments of crisis which will soon befall them.

However, there is a strong and well-developed body of work that emerged from the discipline of psychology to suggest that when the sports performer loses focus on the task and begins to focus more fully on the benefits that accrue because of achievement, their performance inevitably declines. Research by Jackson and Csikszentmihalyi (1999) has sought to explain why this takes place in sport and other perform-ance domains. Based on Csikszentmihalyi's (1975) concept of flow, and related closely to Ravizza's (1977) account of peak experiences in sport, there are sound theoretical accounts of why it is essential that for top performance to be maintained attention should be focused on the task rather than on extrinsic factors.

Managers in this situation must ensure that they keep a clear view of what they have achieved so far and what they must keep doing to succeed in the future. Although this may sound strange, the quality of humility in times of great success may help to prolong these moments of optimal performance and can help prepare the manager to deal with the imminent failure in a balanced and constructive way. The sport psy-chologist will find this task difficult to carry out where the manager has little experience in their job, or where most of that experience has been largely positive or even beyond everyone's expectations. Fortunately, most managers who secure Premier League posts have worked their way through the lower leagues as managers, or have been previously in assistant manager, or senior coaching roles. This inevitably means that the vast majority have experienced the highs and spirit-sapping

88

lows that can be encountered along the way. The sport psychologist will need to draw on the manager's previous experience, including experience as players. Armed with sound theory emanating from the intellectually coherent and vast body of empirical research from psychologists like Csikszentmihalyi (1992) and the applied work of highly experienced and esteemed sport psychologists like Ravizza (2002b), the sport psychologist's role will be to guide the manager to recognize that their most important weapon in this situation is, somewhat paradoxically, humility.

IDENTITY

Maintaining a high degree of humility will ensure that there is less temptation to overreact when a difficult moments arise. The sport psychologist may be involved in meeting the manager during a prolonged difficult phase, where positive results are difficult to come by, and media and fan criticism escalates daily. This will be a critical moment in the manager's career path. Although he may not be in a strong position to influence all the important factors that have contributed to the difficult period the club are currently experiencing, the manager may have an opportunity to decide how the club will portray themselves in public and the mentality they wish to adopt. Such moments test leadership qualities, and, in a deeper sense, highlight the importance of personal identity. In terms of leadership, the hard moments will reveal clearly whether the manager is sure about how he should behave in a crisis and how he can inspire others around him, such as players and their staff.

In order to demonstrate leadership skills in the toughest of times, it is essential that managers know who they are and what they stand for. Although it may appear more philosophical than psychological, the most important task facing the manager is to be able to maintain a position of equilibrium, that is, to be able to react and deal with problems in a constructive way and to avoid overreacting and creating problems where none previously existed. This will depend upon his capacity to maintain a long-term view of the situation facing the team, including with his own career goals and aspirations. It will require a perspective that can acknowledge how often difficult moments eventually right themselves if people continue to do the good things that brought success previously and are prepared to carefully analyse existing practices in order to remove those things that are holding progress back. This requires a set of paradoxical qualities.

Research with 100 top chief executives of US companies, Nobel Prize winners and other exceptional individuals in sport and business carried out by Czikszentmihalyi (1996), revealed that the highest performing leaders possessed a set of common qualities. Despite operating in different environments, these extremely successful people were each able to be both humble and proud of their achievements, capable of acting spontaneously yet recognizing the need for order, and were sensitive to the needs of others whilst still being able to act in a decisive and even ruthless way when required. This set of personal characteristics points to what existential psychologists have described as individuals whose identity is composed of a strong and clear sense of self based on authenticity and sound values. According to Frankl (1984), these values refer to the capacity for hope, that is, to be able to strive for the good or the best, despite finding oneself in often difficult circumstances. The other key aspect Frankl mentioned was that such people often had a deep sense of belief that life was ultimately grounded in some form of meaning greater than themselves.

For Frankl this meaning could be located in a personally held religious faith or spiritual belief, love of the human race, or deep concern for the environment. As far as he was concerned, the most important psychological factor was to be committed to something bigger than the self. Emerging out of this notion of identity it is possible to see clear links to the vital concept of humility. In simple terms, knowing that you are not the most important thing is the most powerful way of reminding a person that they cannot control everything, and neither can they make everything ultimately focus on their own needs and concerns.

For the sport psychologist the way to address these complex psychological and personal qualities and their impact on the current situation will depend on the manager's temperament, values and personality. The psychologist's approach will also be affected by the broader context, which could include the history of the club, expectations that surround it and the prevailing culture of the area within which the club is based.

90

LEADERSHIP

The sport psychologist who approaches this work with the manager in a dispassionate and systematic way is unlikely to achieve anything worthwhile. There are many reasons for this; however, the most important is, arguably, because in this work the focus is directed at the whole person. This means that everything is on the table. Professional goals, career aspirations, personal qualities, and psychological skills must all be considered by the sport psychologist if any progress is to be made.

The sport psychologist can also assist the manager in considering the topic of leadership and associated skills. A considerable amount of research in sport psychology has been carried out to identify the types of leadership skills that are necessary for good coaching practice (Murray and Mann 2001). Some of this work has been especially useful in identifying the skills that can be learned by those wanting to succeed in sport in leadership roles. For example, Murray and Mann identified that effective leaders in sport possess high levels of sport-specific knowledge, charisma, an ability to use rewards and sanctions skilfully, high levels of emotional control and were positive role models. Whilst this research is useful in a range of sporting contexts, some of the findings may not transfer easily into the type of professional sport culture that exists in Premier League football and other elite sport settings.

The traditions of professional football, most certainly in the UK, have ensured that a certain type of leadership style has traditionally been considered to be the norm. One of the key difficulties is that few researchers and even fewer sport psychologists have had sufficient access to professional football and the Premier League in particular to carry out systematic and rigorous research on leadership. However, those who have studied the sport at the highest levels have proposed that one style has been prevalent. The leadership style that appears to have dominated professional football is one that has been based on an authoritarian and dictatorial style, where the players and staff tend to view the leader as someone to be feared and as a strong disciplinarian (Relvas *et al.* 2010). Although not based on in-depth research, there are anecdotal accounts derived from player biographies, the work of journalists and others to suggest that some managers have been able to construct different leadership models about themselves. These individuals are sometimes viewed as charismatic leaders or mavericks, who through the force of their personality and various idiosyncratic attributes have been able to be effective leaders through being persuasive and convincing motivators who have developed close and personal bonds with fans and players.

Within the Premiership the demands are very different from those faced by managers lower down the leagues. The multicultural make-up of the squads, the large backroom staff and the massive financial incentives and media interest in the game mean that the successful leader will need to possess a particular set of skills and qualities. The sport psychologist can help the manager to acquire these by giving them carefully selected reading on good role models from other high performing arenas, such as business and professional sports.

It may also be possible to extract some of the key messages from sport psychology research on the types of skills that can be acquired by managers to enhance their leadership capabilities. One of the most important findings from this literature is that good leaders are not so much born as made (Parker 1996). This is likely to resonate with the many ambitious and highly motivated individuals who are likely to be recruited as managers into the most successful football league in the world.

The sport psychologist can help the development of the manager's leadership skills and qualities. Many managers will have previously been assistant managers at other clubs, or senior coaches and sometimes even team captains during their playing careers. Through these experiences they will already have a high level of skill as leaders. However, the role of manager will undoubtedly require new levels of understanding. This is because of several factors, such as the expectations of other stakeholders regarding how a manager should behave as a leader in professional football, the isolation often associated with this role, and the very public profile that surrounds this function.

The lack of a formal career structure in many professional sports and elite sport organizations will often mean that a person has progressed to a senior position without having either formally or informally spent time developing their knowledge of effective leadership. This situation would be much more unusual to find in public and private sector organizations. In those environments, it is normal practice for staff

92

with a leadership role to receive support through mentoring, pursuing additional education opportunities and working closely with other successful and effective leaders in their own organization or elsewhere (Kuhn and Jackson 2008). In spite of research findings to the contrary, the general consensus in elite and professional sport appears to be that leaders are born. It is also anticipated that individuals will be able to use their leadership skills successfully across a whole wide range of different situations.

Again, there is literature addressing the topic of successful leadership in business organizations that suggests leadership is situation-specific, and that what may be considered excellent leadership in one area of activity is unlikely to be effective in a different area (Fairhurst 2008).

In terms of the particular skills which the manager already possesses or has to acquire quickly to be able to do his job well, the ability to delegate is one of the most important. For some individuals, especially those who have a high level of confidence in their own capabilities, delegation of tasks and of authority is something they may find extremely difficult. The complexity of the manager's role and the scale of demands placed upon them means that they will be incapable of leading the group effectively without being able to delegate a large number of tasks, including those that they would rather carry out themselves. This skill can be acquired and improved.

The sport psychologist has an excellent opportunity to encourage and support the managers in this skill. For example, a sport psychologist could give clear examples of where a failure to fully delegate a task has resulted in problems for the team, causing friction between individuals and a dissipation of energy and motivation. Given the intense pressures and important decisions that managers face daily in a Premiership club or elite sports organization, it is understandable that they would be reluctant to hand over important decisions to other colleagues.

The sport psychologist could highlight the fact that, by delegating certain important decisions, the manager is helping to demonstrate the level of trust in the staff team. In addition, the sport psychologist could draw on examples of good practise in sports management literature or from business management research (e.g. Barker 1999) that confirms how important this type of delegation is to the efficiency of the organization, and to the career development of the leader. This final comment refers to the fact that delegation is absolutely necessary for all who wish to lead, and that the higher someone progresses in their chosen career, the more essential it will be for them to delegate significant amounts of work, and crucially, some important tasks that they themselves would normally wish to do.

Within the world of elite and professional sport, the type of leadership style seems to be usually based on a less democratic and more authoritarian approach. Many managers and leaders in professional sport have an immensely strong work ethic. They have been able to progress their careers in an environment where trust between colleagues and amongst players is much desired and spoken about, but may in fact be less evident in reality. The lack of trust between people, and especially between leaders and those being led, is not exclusive to Premiers League football and elite sport organizations. From an existential psychology perspective, Buber (1958) argued that the self-alienation of our postmodern era, where individuals do not know who they are or what they stand for, will eventually lead to a complete collapse of trust between people, and authentic and honest dialogue will cease completely. It is arguable that some of these tendencies have been taking place across many different kinds of communities in recent years. The level of trust and dialogue between politicians and the electorate in most Western countries currently appears to be moving towards something like this situation. Within the sports organization or football club there is good reason to emphasize the importance of trust.

As one of the most frequently used words in the changing rooms of Premiership football clubs and high-level professional sport, this quality refers to the need to know that others will do their jobs and that they will not knock one another down in the heat of the battle. In some ways, the ultimate definition of an elite sports team could be that it consists of a group of individuals who trust each other completely in order to achieve a singular aim. The sport psychologist could draw on this definition to discuss examples of the strongest sport teams to display these high levels of trust. They can point out that the most important factor in generating this trust is the leadership style and skills of the manager. This significant factor may be difficult for a manager to put in place, despite his understanding and agreeing with it in principle. It is at this

94

point that it is important to remember that leadership depends on skills and the personal qualities of the leader.

The successful leader must have the personal quality of courage. This quality can be seen when a person attempts to do the right thing without being assured that it will lead to the desired outcome. It is this way of describing the courageous act that allows Corlett (1996a), in terms of sport, to base his work on the ideas of Socrates, Aristotle and Aquinas to claim that courage always has a moral component to it. The sport psychologist may be able to help this process by giving the manager articles or extracts from books that explain how important this personal quality is for success at the highest level. Some of the literature about high-achieving individuals in public life, such as politicians, artists, military heroes, sports people and business leaders, can be useful in helping this quality to develop. The sport psychologist may also spend time looking back with the manager at key people they respect as great leaders in their own lives in order to identify courageous behaviour and how this was displayed.

Finally, a high-level manager will undoubtedly have acted courageously at earlier stages of his sporting career, whether as a player or as a coach. By examining what this meant in practice and how he felt about himself at these moments, the manager will potentially grow in this quality, having been able to acknowledge that it is something he has always possessed to some degree and that it is not an abstract 'philosophical' concept or psychological idea, but something that he has experienced at moments of his own life.

Other skills associated with leadership include planning, organization, building teams and group dynamics (Carron and Hausenblas 1998). All these can be improved and the sport psychologist can work with the manager to address each in turn, according to where the biggest need lies. Working on leadership skills can also assist the manager in preparing for his next job. Particularly in the fast-moving and transient world of Premiership football, it is highly important that managers use their experiences to hone their leadership skills to allow them to progress to a bigger job at a more established club. In addition, it must be remembered that the average length of time that a Premiership manager stays in their job is currently around twenty months. This means that it is incumbent on them to develop their leadership skills to assist them to secure a contract extension at their current club or to help them find another post if they are sacked from their present role.

It is important for the manager to acknowledge that leadership is situation-specific. The research on this topic is almost unanimous in suggesting that certain situations will require particular forms of leadership which may be very different from what is required in other environments (Chelladurai and Trail 2006). The sport psychologist can attempt to address this by looking at what kind of leadership would be required to work at a higher level or in a more successful club. Again this can be achieved by discussing the differences that exist in their current leadership role to what they did at a lower league club, with fewer resources and a different mentality. Situation-specific leadership skills are part of this story. As individuals work in more professional environments, where there are greater numbers of specialist staff with high degrees of knowledge and experience, the kind of leadership required within the group may be different from that required in their previous experience. The sport psychologist can help the manager to assess and address the difficulties they might be experiencing because of the different types of leadership skills necessary to guide a large, complex and highly qualified team of specialists.

One of the most powerful methods of demonstrating different leadership styles is to invite high-achieving leaders from business and other sport settings to meet the manager or the senior staff. Indeed, the sport psychologist could suggest that the manager might benefit from a long-term mentorship arrangement with the business leader. There is often a willingness and considerable level of interest from chief executives, directors, company owners and other leaders in the commercial and public sectors to meet and share ideas with managers or the senior staff in top sports organizations. The Premiership club has particular appeal because of the highly political and fast-moving environment within which decisions are often made, and the intense performance focus. Brady *et al.* (2008: 55) have claimed that football has become 'the quintessential model for modern-day talent-dependant business. Football managers have always needed to solve the foremost people management dilemma posed by a new economy increasingly reliant on knowledge workers – how to most effectively manage talent'. In addition, many successful leaders in business, political life and the public sector are passionate about sport and professional football and are highly motivated to understand more about these activities for personal and professional reasons.

The sessions with these individuals could focus explicitly on certain topics that may be especially relevant to the manager at a particular time. For example, the rapid and unexpected success of a club can demand a change in leadership style, and there might be real value in the manager speaking to someone who has successfully dealt with this type of challenge in a non-sport environment. The sport psychologist could also direct the sessions to assist the manager to begin to acquire, or possibly refine and develop, his skills to meet new challenges in the future. These could relate to the manager's current job, or could be focused on future career opportunities.

Although there is an extensive and impressive body of academic literature that addresses effective leadership and building teams (Kremer and Scully 2002), the manager may gain much more from the type of in-depth analysis that can be enjoyed in one-to-one sessions with other experienced practitioners. This has another important advantage, in that these individual meetings will be fully confidential, which can therefore allow both parties to speak openly and frankly about their experiences of leadership within their different occupations and professional environments. In this way, a reciprocal relationship can be developed, ensuring that the manager of an elite professional sport club and the leader of a major non-sport organization will both benefit from hearing about new ideas, methods or approaches to leadership and managing teams.

Finally, the sport psychologist should be in a good position to carry out an audit of the skills and personal qualities that the manager possesses as a leader. This will allow the manager to identify areas for improvement and target opportunities to gain further knowledge and understanding. This can be used to arrange a series of meetings with individuals who are highly respected for running successful organizations using a particular style of leadership. It could also prove useful to speak to other leaders who operate in areas that are less well understood by the manager. For example, in order to work more skilfully and productively with the media it could be helpful for the manager to meet leaders from this industry. Some of the skills and attitudes that they employ in their work could assist the manager in their own dealings with journalists and reporters.

DEALING WITH STRESS AND ANXIETY

There is little doubt that, as with many managers and leaders of multimillion pound business organizations, there is a high level of stress and anxiety that goes with the job. Some of this is related to the fact that, especially in Premier League football and other elite professional sport organizations, the manager can go from being celebrated to being castigated in a short space of time. This decline can be the result of factors outside their control. Injuries to key players, poor decisions by match officials, financial problems due to difficult economic circumstances or even a run of bad luck, can all turn a positive picture into something extremely negative in a relatively short period. The manager may also have contributed to this rapid descent, through selecting the wrong team, making tactical errors, alienating the media and the team's supporters, failing to take advice from staff or even accepting too much guidance from others. These and many other factors can combine in such a way that it is common for a manager to be perceived externally as a competent leader in one part of a season and hugely incompetent later on, only to emerge at the season end as the embodiment of great leadership (yet again!).

Although this rollercoaster experience can take place in business and public sector organizations, it can be argued that the only other comparable environment to this is that of high-level national politics. However, in some ways even this comparison is inadequate, since politicians, even inept and despised ones, may remain in post until election time. Managers of elite professional sports organizations do not usually have this luxury. In a highly results-oriented culture such as the Premier League, managers (and their senior staff) are even under more pressure than players to deliver positive results consistently. In Premier League football, most first team players have contracts lasting between two and four years, and in this sense, have much more job security than managers who may be fired and paid off with relative ease. The back-room staff, especially assistant managers, the senior coaching team and various other more development-focused and specialist staff (such as sport psychologists) are even easier to remove quickly from their posts. It is usual for backroom staff to have a limited amount of job security in comparison with other professionals operating in public sector organizations, or medium- to large-scale private businesses. In addition, it is usual practise that when managers lose their job, a sizeable number of their backroom staff follows them out of the door. This places an additional burden on the manager, and is also another contributing factor in the levels of stress and anxiety they face.

Sport psychologists may find themselves discussing coping skills and looking at how managers deal with the stress and anxiety encountered in their roles. To date, most research in this area has focused on stress and coping skills in relation to sport performers (Nicholls 2008). However, the range of stressors that a manager may face is considerable, and differs from sport performers and players in that much of it relates to factors beyond the game or match itself. Although Woodman and Hardy (2001) have highlighted that organizational stressors are significant for sports performers, and Nesti (2004) suggested that sport psychologists need to be trained in organizational psychology, there are few references within the sport psychology literature to what managers have to contend with within their roles. Although some of the coping skills reported by Nichols *et al.* may be useful for the manager, it is more likely that the most effective support from the sport psychologist in this situation will relate to an educational intervention aimed at examining the nature of stress and anxiety and discussing specific psychological accounts of these concepts.

The sport psychologist may also be able to support the manager in dealing with stress and anxiety by engaging in a counselling-based session where an attempt is made to examine current experiences, reflect on similar past experience and, crucially, identify how this can be successfully addressed in the future.

Sport psychology literature addressing anxiety has been dominated by cognitive-behavioural and trait psychology based approaches (Nesti 2004). Nesti and Sewell (1999) have criticized this over-reliance on only two psychological approaches to this important concept. The sport psychology research during the past twenty-five to thirty years is also seriously limited in scope because attention has been devoted only to competitive anxiety (Jones 1995). Nesti and Littlewood (in press) have highlighted that this has held back an understanding of the potential for anxiety to be conceived as a positive sign and has ignored the psycho-analytic and existential psychology approaches arguing that anxiety pervades all experiences in life, not just those related to competition per se.

Managers in professional football will undoubtedly experience this type of anxiety as they attempt to fulfil their role as people who must make important decisions daily and find the mental strength to face the consequences when they make the wrong choices.

5

CREATING AND MANAGING THE ENVIRONMENT

Professional sports teams frequently mention the importance of group cohesion and team dynamics. During difficult periods of a season it is not unusual to find a renewed interest in creating team spirit within a professional football team. Within the highly pressured and volatile environment of professional team sport, the concept of team spirit is a frequently used term. This chapter will describe how a manager, support staff and the sport psychologist can be involved in developing team and individual spirit. Before discussing how this can be achieved it is important to clarify what is meant by this contentious term. Watson and Nesti (2005) claimed that despite being one of the most frequently used terms in sport, especially at high-performance levels, there seems to be little discussion of spirit or spiritual dimensions within the sport psychology literature. We will examine some of the reasons for this apparent omission and suggest why it is important for sport psychologists to become more familiar with this term and acknowledge its importance in their applied work.

A further aim of this chapter is to consider the role that the sport psychologist can play in enhancing team cohesion and group processes. This can be addressed through formal mechanisms and structures, or may be effectively dealt with by more informal means. There is little doubt that developing a sound team ethos and a strong team spirit will be a key role for the manager and his coaching staff. Because of the difficulty in getting prolonged access to professional sports environments or a Premiership football team, there is little general literature in sport psychology or within sport psychology research that discusses this topic.

However, early work by Carron and Hausenblas (1988) on team dynamics and cohesion, and Chelladurai and Trail (2006) on leadership and leadership styles, has been used in studies from within other sporting contexts. Some of this work applies easily and readily to the world of professional sport and Premiership football. However, many of the models that have been proposed in relation to group processes and team dynamics are largely incapable of capturing some of the unique factors that exist within a Premiership football environment or professional football club.

Many clubs engage the services of a chaplain to provide support to players, their families and the staff over several seasons. These individuals offer pastoral support, and, where players or staff are interested or have a particular need, they can give spiritual guidance and religious advice. As a sport psychologist working in Premiership football I have found that many players react positively to the availability to this type of support. Professional football, especially at Premiership levels, is now an increasingly multicultural environment, with players from a vast array of different ethnic, national and cultural groups. Players' religious beliefs can range across a large number of different faiths and traditions.

The work carried out by a chaplain may at first appear quite distanced from the performance-focused agenda of a sport psychologist. However, depending on the approach that the sport psychologist draws upon, the chaplain can become an important ally in furthering their work. This will be examined through the inclusion of two short vignettes that reveal how the development of the human spirit and of players' religious spirituality can be important in creating an optimal environment for elite sport performance.

An important task of the sport psychologist in professional team sport must be to help performers and their support staff maintain their freshness, vitality, capacity to innovate, courage, honesty and authenticity. These personal qualities can be developed through careful use of skills and can be learned and enhanced through sport psychology support. These terms are frequently used when coaches are discussing the need to maintain an optimum performance state during the demanding rigours of a season. The sport psychologist can assist the emergence or re-emergence of these qualities through a process of individual and

102

collective renewal. In many ways the task is never-ending. Nevertheless, it may be important to use different approaches and techniques from time to time to help people to start again after disappointments, failures and defeat.

Finally, a theme running throughout this chapter will relate to the communication style that dominates within Premiership football and professional football clubs in the UK. Although this may be changing given the significant increase in overseas players and foreign managers, there is a particular and traditional way of communicating that must be understood by sport psychologists who hope to succeed in this milieu. Commonly referred to as 'banter', this has been studied in relation to military settings, and has been acknowledged as something that features strongly in the majority of professional sports. At its simplest, banter describes a direct, and at times personally abrasive, form of communication, where often serious and important points can be made within a humorous context.

DEVELOPING HUMAN SPIRIT

The concept of spirit and spirituality has received considerable attention in mainstream psychology, particularly within approaches that are based on a holistic perspective. For example, humanistic, transpersonal and existential psychology paradigms are open to the notion of spirituality since they conceive of human persons as being constituted of mind, body and spirit. Cognitive, behavioural and psychoanalytic perspectives have no place for spirit and spirituality within their approaches. The reasons for this have been discussed within a sporting context by Nesti (2007), who has argued that where psychology is conceived as being closely related to the natural sciences it is unable to accommodate philosophically sounding terms such as spirit, spirituality, passion and courage. This does present a dilemma for sport psychologists who are only prepared to work from a cognitive or behavioural perspective in professional football where these words are used frequently.

Nesti (2007) has pointed out that this obstacle has not prevented some individuals from attempting to improve team spirit despite basing their professional work on psychological approaches that do not recognize words like spirit or spirituality. In some cases, sport psychologists have tried to get around this inconsistency by translating the term spirit to mean confidence, or sometimes even motivation. However, in my experience this will not be acceptable to players and most staff working in high-level sports, including Premiership football. These individuals are often extremely clear that spirit refers to something *other* than motivation, confidence or mental toughness, and that they have sound empirical reasons for making this claim.

Pieper (1995) has usefully made the distinction between human spirit and religious spirituality. Although both are seen within many traditions and theological accounts as being inseparable, it is possible to speak of a humanist spirit without recourse to religious terminology.

Within a professional football club there is much talk about the importance of team spirit. This quality is considered so important that managers and their coaches devote considerable efforts to enhancing and developing this quality within their teams. This often takes the form of team-building activities that place players and staff in demanding and sometimes extreme environments. For example, as a sport psychologist working in Premiership football, I have been involved in organizing outdoor adventure programmes in mountainous terrain and choosing a range of activities to force individuals to have experiences well outside their comfort zones. On occasion, specialist instructors have been employed to teach the players about watercraft skills, abseiling, rock climbing and other similar tasks. These are designed to demonstrate the importance of trust between individuals and are deliberately structured to ensure that individuals have to respond to new situations and push themselves beyond their previous limits. These and other experiences of a more cerebral and less physical nature, such as visits to different cultures and attending unusual events, help to take players out of their normal ways of thinking and behaving. The range of activities that can be used to develop team spirit range from the physically and mentally arduous, such as training with the army for several days during the pre-season, to more sedate activities, such as going to the theatre or visiting an art gallery.

It has long been accepted that physically challenging, and mentally and emotionally demanding experiences can be used to generate spirit within individuals and across teams. This approach to the concept of spirit is in keeping with definitions provided by Pieper (1989). In agreeing with this, Nesti (2007) suggests that spirit is most usually seen and valued when individuals or groups have to continue to pursue a task when they are in a state of mental, emotional and physical exhaustion. One of the major reasons that Premiership football clubs and other sports teams are keen to pay for specialists to run team-building activities is their ability to create artificial opportunities for such moments to occur.

There is often an expectation that the sport psychologist will be an expert in providing a variety of experiences that might be specifically planned and structured to increase the likelihood that team spirit will be enhanced. It can prove useful if the sport psychologist has previous experience of collaborating with some of the highly skilled and professional companies currently operating in the outdoor education and outdoor adventure market.

The evaluation of team-building events and their relationship to players' performance in matches and at training is difficult to assess in a neat and tidy way. Coaches, managers and others usually talk about 'feeling' that people have engaged and stretched themselves. They often comment that you can sense the spirit in the group or in particular individuals, during, and after, a successful team-building experience.

Spirit can also be developed and created by a variety of events and moments that do not involve discomfort, hardship or sacrifice. Listening to speakers with powerful and inspirational stories from their lives, attending social activities, including meals together, changing daily routines, listening to music and even sitting together as staff and players at meal times, can all be used to generate a positive spirit within the group. Managers and coaches are convinced that these and other similar initiatives can bring huge benefits and lead to improved performance of the group and of individuals within it.

In my experience, there is considerable resistance from managers, coaches and others to describe increases in team spirit in terms of stronger motivation, enhanced confidence or greater mental toughness (Thelwell *et al.* 2005). Unfortunately, few empirical studies exist within the literature on this topic, and to date no research has been carried out within professional team sport environments where the concept of spirit is pervasive.

However, the players and professional football clubs that I have worked with are convinced that all these broad types of activities in one way or another are capable of impacting deeply on their sense of self and views of others.

The spirit of a team or individual is a much discussed topic within the media and is sometimes assumed to be the key quality possessed by the most successful professional football teams. The belief of many coaches, players and managers at the highest level of the game is that teams and players with lots of spirit will be able to overcome the odds and persist in the face of great difficulty. The fact that most in sport psychology seem ill-prepared to deal with this topic, or, even more problematically, question its very existence (Crust 2007), could lead to great difficulties for sport psychologists hoping to work in this culture.

Many Premiership football staff and players, in common with other elite-level sport performers, talk about how they have experienced playing in teams with fantastic spirit and describe how this has brought an added dimension to their performances over a season or particular period of time. Their rich descriptions of this concept, how it can be developed, and its importance to performance, is surely something that warrants serious consideration from researchers within sport psychology. A qualitative methodological approach is most likely to be able to capture this data in a rigorous, valid and meaningful way. This is because qualitative methods are ideally suited to the analysis of subjective moments and individual experiences across a variety of activities including sport (Sparkes 2002).

TEAM BUILDING

The factors associated with creating a cohesive and high-performing team have been extensively considered by organizational psychologists and sport psychologists for many years. In addition, there is a large group of individuals and organizations who operate within the corporate sector and possess expertise in the area of building teams. These

106

consultants are specialists in identifying improvements in processes and communication systems and have made a significant impact on companies operating in diverse fields. Much of this work is especially relevant to the sport psychologist operating within elite-level and professional sport. Breakdowns in communication at all levels in sports organizations and teams can lead to underachievement and failure.

The work of management specialists and organizational theorists like Gilson *et al.* (2001) represents one of the most powerful series of accounts provided by business consultants on the team-building practices of sport teams. Their work looked closely at a number of world-class and established sports organizations, such as the New Zealand All Blacks, Bayern Munich, McLaren F1 and the Chicago Bulls. Unlike most of the published literature within sport psychology, this research took place at some of the most professional and high-achieving sports teams in the world. It involved researchers immersing themselves in each culture for months at a time, in order to examine processes closely from the inside. This work is rarely cited by sport psychologists in their research into leadership, team dynamics or group processes, yet it is an extremely important contribution to the field. In my work as a sport psychologist operating at Premiership football clubs, and based on my close association with others who have adopted similar roles during the past ten years, there is considerable enthusiasm for the literature provided by Gilson *et al.*

This is somewhat ironic given that the five individuals I am referring to have all studied sport psychology to at least master's degree level at highly ranked UK universities. For these sport psychologists, unfortunately, the reality of supporting team building and strengthening communication processes within Premiership football are far removed from the research findings that are published in the sport psychology journals.

The sport psychologist in this environment may be faced with carrying out certain tasks for which they are often rather poorly prepared as a result of their academic qualifications and skill base. The tasks can involve establishing an organizational system that identifies interdepartmental relationships and clarifies roles and responsibilities. They may also find themselves preparing job descriptions and establishing a system of monitoring and evaluation of performance and developing and putting in place a systematic review process for staff and players. The sport psychologist can make an important contribution to the success and overall performance of the staff and the players through setting up a systematic and planned approach to communication.

It is often the case that within Premiership football clubs there are a few established structures and agreed policies that govern communication between individuals, departments and staff and players. All these activities can help the process of team building. They will go a long way to ensuring that a cohesive staff imbued with spirit is there to offer loyal and consistent support to the manager and the players no matter how arduous the journey.

PROVIDING A CLUB CHAPLAIN

The presence of a chaplain is commonplace in many elite professional sports organizations. Although these individuals typically operate on a voluntary basis, unlike other staff in this environment, they can provide an important form of pastoral support to players, staff and their families. It may appear strange that such individuals would devote time to such a small group, given the demands typically placed on most clergy with busy parishes to run.

The role of a chaplain can work on a number of different levels within a club. In terms of supporting the players, it can be argued that on occasion some of the chaplain's work closely resembles that of a sport psychologist (Watson and Nesti 2005). This is particularly the case where the sport psychologist adopts a counselling psychology approach in some of their work with the players. It is on these occasions, and especially when dealing with matters other than mental skills, that there may be an opportunity for the sport psychologist and the chaplain to work closely together.

As has been suggested (Nesti 2007), the professional practice of these two different vocations often have much in common. For example, there is great importance placed in both forms of support on the issues of confidentiality, trust and taking a long-term view where this is feasible and desirable.

In my experience, where the chaplain is highly visible around the club and at the training ground it becomes easier for players to seek this individual out when they are experiencing a broad range of pastoral problems, especially those relating to family and relationships. The player may not wish to speak with the sport psychologist about these concerns, possibly because they would like a different perspective on them. Although players vary greatly in their understanding of the role of sport psychologists, most would expect that they are more performance-focused than the club chaplain.

Nevertheless, a belief in the neat and apparently clean separation between performance in training and matches and the type of support available from a chaplain echoes the misunderstandings that exist within sport psychology itself. As has been examined in Chapter 3, Nesti and Littlewood (2009) have challenged the idea that sport psychology should either be exclusively focused on mental skills or that it should follow the suggestions of Andersen (2009) and avoid considering anything relating to performance-based issues.

Club chaplains are usually very knowledgeable and passionate about football and sport in general. They work in the game on a voluntary basis to meet the spiritual needs of players and staff and to provide pastoral care. Whilst they are concerned with matters of the spirit and religious belief, it is usual to find that, as the sport psychologist, they also believe that people facing difficulties and pain will often struggle to meet the performance demands of their roles.

For professional or high-level sport performers, a major way of achieving self-fulfilment is through performing well in their job. The chaplain, like the sport psychologist, can be a form of support for players attempting to achieve this in their professional lives.

The following example reveals how a player might benefit from working with a chaplain and how this could also assist the role of the sport psychologist.

There are opportunities throughout the season for the chaplain to sit down and offer confidential support to players during difficult periods.

Sometimes this happens when a player is facing a critical moment involving a significant change to their circumstances. These changes can appear suddenly and quite unexpectedly at times.

In the following example, a player was attempting to deal with the serious illness of a close relative, and was currently out of the team despite being fit and available for selection. The chaplain had already met this player quite informally during the last two previous seasons at the club. The sport psychologist had been working in the pre-season and first phase of the competitive programme to address issues related to this player's lack of confidence when in goal-scoring positions and his tendency towards harsh self-criticism. In addition, this player tended to view his situation as evidence that the manager did not like him personally and that he selected his favourites instead of him. Although the player did not possess a clear understanding of the role of the chaplain at the club, he respected the chaplain as an individual of integrity and good common sense.

Although he had been brought up in a family where Catholic beliefs and practices were important, the player was not a practising Catholic. Nor was the chaplain a Catholic, but belonged to another Christian denomination. The player was vaguely aware of this fact, although his understanding of the differences between Christian denominations and between other faiths was poor. The chaplain had met the sport psychologist from time to time to discuss some of the shared issues that emerged from their short meetings with the player. These took place in both an informal and more formal way at the training ground and around the club in general. The dialogue below attempts to capture this type of work and seeks to illuminate how the work of the sport psychologist can benefit from close cooperation with the club chaplain.

> The player came in to training at his usual time, and, as was his habit, went over to the serving counter in the dining room to make some breakfast. He was always one of the first to arrive to training and usually sat in a quiet part of the dining room on his own as he ate breakfast.
>
> The sport psychologist and the chaplain had organized an early morning meeting to take place over coffee in the dining room. They

were discussing the general mood of the camp and sharing concerns about particular players and staff where this was appropriate and ethical to do so. The player looked over and acknowledged the chaplain and the sport psychologist. Such acknowledgement is important in many ways. One of the most valuable is that the players and staff can see the level of professional respect that existed between chaplain and psychologist, which in turn can enhance the perception that players have about the value of each of these specialists. It can also be a powerful visible expression of beliefs about the link between pastoral support and sporting performance.

Seeing the opportunity to speak to the player in private, the chaplain moved over towards the corner of the dining room to where he was sitting. At this point, the sport psychologist got up and left to go to his office in another part of the building.

'You're in early,' said the chaplain.

'I always like to get in before the rest of the lads, it means I get the choice of the best cereals and I get some peace to eat my breakfast,' joked the player.

'How is it going for you at the moment? I see you have not had a lot of starts or even got in the squad this season. That must be really tough to deal with especially when we need players with your experience to push people on,' said the chaplain.

The chaplain gently eased himself into a chair placed at the side of the breakfast table.

'How are things going with your friend who was very ill? Did you manage to go over to visit him last week as you mentioned, or was it just too hectic in the end?'

As the player frowned and hesitated for a moment the chaplain sat in silence and allowed the player the time to consider his thoughts.

'I feel really bad that I never got over, although I have sent a text and left messages, and phoned his wife several times to see how they are doing. I feel a bit guilty to be honest, I know what it's like because my dad had something similar and I remember that during that time I couldn't think straight, and I was really angry and frustrated. I suppose I have not tried hard enough to be really truthful because I am having a pretty crap time here myself.'

The player left the final statement hanging in the air almost waiting to be picked up and answered in some way or other.

'You have at least tried, despite having a difficult time yourself, said the chaplain. You must not be too hard on yourself – this is what it's like when we care about someone. We never think we do enough. Maybe though, there are other things that we could do that would help. It just doesn't mean that you have to speak to that person, but maybe it would help his wife or even with something small for his parents or the children, because I know you are really close friends and he will know that you really care.'

The player looked at the chaplain with a mixture of embarrassment, relief and hesitation.

'I know I shouldn't really say this, but I don't think that I am able to be that useful for him or his family because I am having such a tough time here at the club at the moment. It's really hard to think properly about others, even good mates who I really care about, when I'm having such an ugly time myself.'

The chaplain knew that the player was beginning to consider how he could address his own problems without feeling he was being disloyal to his close friend. The chaplain continued discussing the types of small things that the player could do in a practical way that might help his ill friend. After discussing this for several minutes he changed focus to the player himself and his own happiness.

'You know your friend would want you to do some of the things we've been chatting about, especially where these give a little help to his family, but you also know that he would not want you to do anything at the expense of your own work and responsibilities to yourself. Without trying to get yourself back on the right track, you will not be able to help others as much as you would like.'

The chaplain looked at the player and knew that he understood fully what he had just said.

'You mean I need to stop moping about and get my act together to force my way back into this team.'

The player did not say much more to the chaplain beyond this but thanked him for speaking to him and finished by saying that he knew he had to act rather than waiting for things to happen. Later on that day the chaplain and the sport psychologist met for a catch up in relation to two other players who were new to the team and were having various difficulties settling into British culture. Both of these players had strong religious beliefs and they were finding it difficult to fit in to the dominant secular atmosphere that prevails in our culture. Both individuals had responded by throwing themselves into community and church-based activities that were associated with their particular faiths. The chaplain discussed how these activities had been completely welcomed by their local faith groups, and that the players seemed to be feeling more integrated than when they both arrived on their loans at the start of the season.

The conversation then turned to the player that the chaplain had briefly met in the dining room at breakfast time.

'He is a really good lad, with good values and he cares about other people, but he seems to really be struggling about addressing his own problems here in the club,' said the chaplain. He continued, 'You know, or maybe you didn't, that he is really close to his friend David who is really is having a difficult time and his family likewise with this illness. I think I need to see him regularly because he is very flat at the moment and is so down on himself.'

'This doesn't surprise me,' said the sport psychologist. 'One of the real difficulties of getting him to stick to the work we are doing to help his performances is that he can be incredibly harsh and brutally unfair on himself at times. I know that psychologically speaking this is his technique to avoid having to take responsibility and to move forward despite knowing that some of the problems and difficulties he faces are due to his own failings, whilst others are external to him. Statements made by many sport psychologists about controlling the controllables make great sense for the situation he is in. However, in my experience, before some players can do this they need to accept where they are genuinely responsible for their lack of progress and be clear about the things that they do not have any influence over. This takes courage because it is about facing up to the truth of the situation. When you lack a deep level of self-belief because you really do not know who you are then it is extremely difficult for you to begin to take these steps, and the easier option is to blame others and to dismiss yourself as completely unworthy. I am really glad that you have met him at this time because, although this sounds terrible, I don't want him to use his friend's illness as another excuse not to attempt to fulfil himself. The saving grace with this player is that he has real ability and that there is tangible evidence of this – he played so well last season and during earlier stages in his career. Sometimes you can lose yourself and for some personalities it will take a long time to get back. When he gets a chance in the team, if he is not psychologically prepared and in the right place, he could suffer a great setback that would make the work with him even harder to move forward. I think that with both of us keeping up a consistent level of support and helping him to stay on the task and not look for quick and easy solutions we will help him get back to who he can really be.'

'Do you think I should tell the manager about all of this?' said the chaplain. 'It's just that I am not sure they know about how close he is and how upset he is about the situation. Obviously I would want to ask the player about this, but maybe even without his consent it is important for his welfare and progress for the manager to know something about this. I think we need to have a deep conversation with him together, to explain how as a chaplain to the club and sport psychologist we have a unified view based on our different expertise

114

> and knowledge about how best to support him. I think we can do this without revealing details that should remain confidential between us and the player; however, the manager needs to be aware of this and equally important, know that we are working closely with the player and that some of the work we do and the tasks for the player to follow through on will be less effective without the active support of the manager and of senior coaching staff.'

This vignette reveals that there are critical moments in a player's career where spiritual, pastoral and sport performance-related concerns are interwoven. Such a perspective is consistent with the holistic approach to sport psychology as advocated over three decades ago by Martens (1979) who reminded applied sport psychologists that they needed to work with the person first and the athlete second. This view is consistent with an existential psychology approach which has always proposed, in addition to Martens's point, that it must also be remembered that the person should be understood as an individual located within a community and a culture. From this it follows that in order to understand sport performers it will not be enough to merely examine their psychological approach to performance. Instead, the sport psychologist must consider their lives as a whole (Nesti and Sewell 1999).

HUMAN SPIRIT AND RELIGIOUS SPIRITUALITY

What follows is an account based on various meetings that took place with Premiership players in the three clubs I have worked with during the past eight years and meetings with professional players during the seven years before this. The sessions were traditional sport psychology meetings in the sense that the focus was on helping the performer to improve as a professional footballer. As has been explained in Chapter 2, the approach I adopt to my practice is to consider all aspects of an individual's life as being relevant to how he carries out his role as professional sport performer.

The situation that I am describing here makes the important distinction between human spirituality and religiously derived accounts of this concept. The approach taken to my work with professional footballers over the past fifteen years has been undoubtedly influenced by the views expressed by players on a number of issues. Some of these are centred on their understanding of the work of a sport psychologist. Others revolve around how they are able to assess their psychological and emotional state and the confidence they have in discussing this with someone they may not know that well. However, maybe more surprisingly for some sport psychologists, professional footballers have frequently spoken to me about their religious beliefs and notions of human spirit.

Although the language and terminology used by players can be different, reflecting the cultural, ethnic, national and other differences between them, there are some common themes that emerge. One of these relates to how important the player sees their religious beliefs in helping them to perform successfully in the demanding environment of professional football. At other times, dialogue has centred on important topics such as the person's values and beliefs, which allow them to maintain the standards they expect of themselves, irrespective of the difficulties they may face. At these times, players frequently talk about the importance of their family and the commitments they have to ideals or particular causes. Often they mention their love of the game.

Discussion about this concept usually does not focus on abstract arguments about whether love is solely an emotional response, a product of eros or a human strategy for survival. More usually, the player, consistent with the ideas of Polanyi (1958), assumes that the sport psychologist will know what love refers to through their own personal knowledge and shared human nature. This love of football can be best explained from a psychological perspective by drawing on Deci and Ryan's (1985) work on motivation. They defined intrinsically motivated behaviour as actions done for rewards inherent within a task. These rewards are said to be related to feelings of self-determination and perceived competence.

All of this may still sound far removed from the narrow performance-focused remit of the sport psychologist. I hope that the following accounts will reveal that this represents a misunderstanding and may even be a biased perspective reflecting the discomfort that many in sport psychology have with words like spirit, spirituality and religious belief.

116

The meeting described in the following vignette took place at a location away from the training ground. This was to ensure that the session could take place in an atmosphere of complete privacy and confidentiality.

> I sat down on the chair in the room and waited for the player to come to the room for our planned meeting. He had agreed three days earlier to meet at this time and that we would set aside between half an hour to an hour for our session. When the player had sat down he immediately began to describe his thoughts and feelings about the current challenge he was facing. The player started by saying that something was not as it should be, and he wanted to tell the sport psychologist to make sure that his perspective was the right one and discuss how he could address this issue.
>
> Player: 'I am having a really bad time at the moment but I can't believe how quickly some people, especially amongst the staff, appear to change how they see things. For me it is so important that we do everything we can as individuals and as part of this family, which is what our team is meant to be, to communicate properly with each other especially when we are up against the wall. Some people here could lose their jobs; some good people are under great pressure for doing the right thing. I see a real lack of respect. We should be respecting people rather than just viewing each other as a means to an end. This is not how I run my life. I know sometimes I can be guilty of treating other people as vehicles to be used and as things that can help me get success. But I very rarely do this because this is wrong! Am I right to say to a psychologist that something is wrong even though I can understand why people may do this?'
>
> Sport psychologist: 'No, it is acceptable for you to say that some behaviours, thoughts, or ideas are wrong. You are acknowledging that sometimes you are guilty of the same actions but you are also prepared to accept that you are right to feel guilt because these actions are wrong. This relates to your values, and deepest held beliefs which in turn influence, guide and inform your psychological perspective, and how you attempt to deal with events.

'For many sport psychologists who work from a holistic approach in psychology it is absolutely consistent and logical to recognize that the philosophy of life you possess is closely related to your mental attitude and the psychological approach you use to pursue your goals – how else could I claim that, as I told you when we first met, I work with you as a person, which means everything that you feel is important about your identity, and about who you are, must be considered, as I am here in my role to support and serve you. The aim is always to help you to fulfil yourself, to achieve more, to grow, or in the words of sport and psychology, to perform better more often! Why else would you sit down and tell me these things in my role as a sport psychologist if you didn't think that they were in some way connected? But now that you mention your values and beliefs, maybe we should talk about what these are, and how they work in your life, and maybe even why they are so important to you?'

Player: 'I have worked with two sport psychologists before and they both pointedly told me that they could not discuss these matters with me, and they suggested I speak to the club chaplain or my religious leader. I do speak to those people and they are often very helpful and bring real perspective into my life. However, as a sport psychologist I expect you are not afraid to hear me talk about why I think we need to change our culture and values at the moment at the club. I know that this is difficult for you or me to do alone, but it is important for me to say these things nevertheless. To be honest and truthful, ultimately, I only fully accept judgement on who I am and how well I fulfil my obligations as a person and a professional footballer from one person. That person is God. I know you must know this because of the conversations you have with the guys and the players you have worked with before. You see, for many of us, just knowing that God is always there as a permanent and consistent person in our lives is a wonderful source of peace, and gives us great strength to carry on in difficult times. The incredible lack of respect and inconsistency of treatment that seems so much a part of playing in professional football can break so many people in my opinion. I know of players who are fragile and almost broken in their core, and despite the constant banter they give and take they are frightened and scared. No one sees this in the outside world, and even these close to the players can seem to miss it. But their fellow players who live in the same world can spot it! Some try to find a way out through addictions like gambling, drugs or alcohol abuse. Lots just bravely soldier on, but they are really only one step away from disaster. When you receive so much so quickly in terms of wealth, fame and honour and yet know that this can be taken away in an instant through injury, a lack of form or when people stop believing in you it's tougher than some people think! It means that you can be taken over by forces outside of your control if you are not strong, have good values and beliefs. For me having a strong set of values and a morality based on my religious beliefs helps me to stay true to myself, and not to overreact to either of these extreme positive or negative scenarios. It is important to me as a player with these beliefs to know that you respect the work of our club chaplain and that you are prepared to acknowledge that those of us who have a religious belief are not weak or strange! I wonder how many of the staff realize how many of the players are deeply committed to their religious beliefs? It seems that they don't know what to say about it. They must realize surely in the first team squad that we have three Muslim players who are committed to their faith, and at least six Christian players for whom their beliefs are absolutely central to who they are and how they try to behave. They seem to have forgotten that the Premiership is full of players from all around the world and that many of us come from countries with strong and living religious traditions. We do not expect the staff to subscribe to our religious convictions, but we are surprised that many seem unaware of their importance in our lives. As I said, when this is also the case with sport psychologists, given that their role must surely be to work with us irrespective our beliefs, then the matter is even more amazing!'

Sport psychologist: 'I know that you are not telling me these things and expecting that I will engage in some kind of advanced theological discussion on the merits of Islam or the differences between various denominations within Christianity, but that you are telling me about the central component of your identity, the most fundamental source of meaning in your life and that your religious beliefs and the values associated with them lead you in a particular direction in terms of how you are dealing with what you see as the inconsistent communication and lack of personal respect that you and others are experiencing at the moment. Can you tell me about how you are able to draw on your religious faith to help you to be fully yourself, and maintain the best performance focus you can despite the very negative and unhelpful environment at present?'

The sport psychologist can help to create an environment where the club chaplain is fully a part of the support team. Because of the increasing numbers of professional players, especially at the highest levels, who declare that their religious beliefs are central to their identity and therefore crucial in the way they deal with the psychological demands of their sport, it is essential that this is acknowledged and accepted by all support staff at the club.

WHEN THE BANTER STOPS

Although banter can have a positive effect on communication within the group, there are moments when it can have a negative and destructive impact. For example, sometimes it can be used to protect the group from outsiders, educate newcomers and ensure compliance from those who threatening team cohesion, or it can be used as a method of dealing with intense personal and organizational stress.

Banter within a Premiership football environment or a professional football club can be a remarkably powerful and positive tool that enables a close and trusting relationship to exist in a demanding set of conditions. At other times, it can be used unconsciously, as a way to punish or coerce individuals. It also has the potential to evolve into a mechanism for bullying and can become a deeply dysfunctional method of avoiding genuine and honest dialogue.

Over the course of a season, there are frequent occasions where the amount of banter diminishes between individuals and may even disappear altogether, at least temporarily. During these moments the sport psychologist is presented with both a serious challenge and an opportunity to build new patterns of communication that will facilitate greater openness and honesty, which may have previously been miss-ing. In this sense, banter in Premiership football and professional sports environments is occasionally used as a technique by individuals, or a strategy by groups, to avoid confronting the reality of a difficult situ-ation. It has been noted that soldiers in battle conditions use banter in an effort to maintain positive communication, keep up their spirits and as a technique to attempt to alleviate the effects of stress and anxiety (May 1977). Within a Premiership football club, moments such as facing possible relegation matches, games that must be won to save jobs and careers and dealing with massive negative media coverage can have a deleterious effect on communication within the team and cause a rift between staff and players. The sport psychologist will be in an import-ant position at this point and needs to be aware of serious failures in communication between players and staff, the manager and their staff, or players and the manager.

A lack of clear and open communication can be a sign that individuals are withdrawing, pulling back into themselves, and away from others. This is often done from self-protection, whether it be staff fearing for their futures and their jobs or players who do not wish to be moved on or sold. This can also lead to a form of social loafing where individu-als attempt to hide within the group in the hope that they will survive until better times. All these antics and others are likely to make a dire situation even worse. Sport psychologists will need all their skills and personal qualities to begin to address communication problems of this type; crucially, they will need the full support of the manager, other key staff, and possibly the chairman and club owners as they attempt to renew these processes.

6

THE LIAISON OFFICER

INTRODUCTION

The liaison officer may be an individual or a group of individuals who have the responsibility to assist players with a range of non-football related concerns. These may involve the player's immediate family and can have a significant impact on how well a player settles into a new environment, deals with a change in circumstance and handles specific unforeseen problems. The formal duties of a typical liaison officer will be discussed in this chapter. We will examine how their role can assist the performance of the player, and consider how this work can relate to that of the sport psychologist.

Although the post of liaison officer is frequently found at the highest levels of professional sport, the work can be effectively carried out by a number of people such as the club secretary, senior coaching staff and the sport psychologist in situations where there is no single post holder dealing with these matters. The skill of this work is as much determined by how the players respond to this support service as it is to the existence of agreed and formal job descriptions. Another important influence on the type of work that can be carried out is the degree to which the manager empowers the liaison officer to engage in particular tasks.

SUPPORTING THE SPORT PSYCHOLOGIST

The sport psychologist may have an excellent opportunity to develop a close working relationship with the liaison officer. Such a relationship may improve access to some players and allow the sport psychologist to be more involved in providing support for family and friends, and meeting important people in the player's life. All of this can help develop a stronger and more open relationship between the sport psychologist and player, and may also increase support for sport psychology work from important individuals who are close to the player in personal and professional terms, such as wives, girlfriends, parents and agents.

The specific tasks of the liaison officer can include family support, assisting players from overseas to settle into new environments and cultures, and ensuring that player lifestyle is consistent with what is necessary for success in a high performance-focused professional sport. Some players will need constant support and attention in relation to their public persona and managing themselves in the media in particular. The sport psychologist and liaison officer can work closely together on media training for players, and the liaison officer can help players unfamiliar with the role of the sport psychologist to understand this role more fully. Beyond their official and public tasks, the liaison officer can provide an excellent source of information in relation to the moods, attitude and psychological state of the players they know best. This information may be based on general observations and the ordinary dealings that the liaison officer has with the players. Such useful background information can assist sport psychologists in directing their work to meet particular demands and challenges that a player may be facing, especially when these arise from issues outside the club.

The liaison officer may also benefit and support players by being able to ask the sport psychologist for advice and guidance in relation to a range of topics. For example, it may be that the liaison officer is aware that a player is having great difficulty in settling in to the club and he is lacking confidence because he is unsure of what is expected of him. A liaison officer who already has a close working relationship with a player may be better placed than the sport psychologist to begin to help the player to address these concerns; unlike the sport psychologist, the liason officer may not be seen as a threat, or viewed as someone close to performance issues and the coaching team.

Where liaison staff or officers have a good understanding of the culture of Premiership football and has extensive knowledge of the club's history, identity and that of the town or city where the team is based, they can have a beneficial effect on a new player. This is particularly pronounced when a player comes from a very different culture and is struggling to understand the practices and values at the club or in broader society. The existence of skilled and experienced liaison officers in Premiership clubs attests to the fact that much of the stress that top-level sport performers have to deal with is not related to playing and narrow performance-based issues. This has been observed by many of the sport psychologists who have worked in elite and professional team sports environments during the past two decades. Unfortunately, this fact has rarely been discussed in the peer-reviewed sport psychology journals with the exception of Rotella's (1990) account of professional baseball. In terms of in-depth theoretically informed books about sport psychology delivery in elite professional team sport, little exists in the field with the exception of Nesti (2004). This is because so few sport psychologists based in academic institutions have been able to gain long-term access to high-level team professional sport. The sport psychologists who have worked extensively in these environments generally do not write about their experiences. This is because of time pressures, restrictions associated with getting work published in academic peer-reviewed journals and because they no longer find sport psychology research useful in guiding their work (personal communication). Interestingly, a small number of researchers in sport psychology (Woodman and Hardy 2001) have caught up with practice and have been able to verify what is already known by coaches, sport performers and sport psychologists working in top-level and professional sports. They have pointed out that organizational sources of stress often represent the most important stressors facing sport performers in a range of environments.

Overall though, this appears to be yet another unfortunate example of where the narrow approaches that have dominated academic sport psychology have driven applied research. The subsequent lack of ecological validity of much that is published in peer-reviewed sport psychology journals means that those entering practice are frequently highly critical of what they have been exposed to during their educational formation in the discipline. For example, one of the most experienced applied sport psychologists in professional football in the world, Mike Forde,

Director of Football Operations at Chelsea FC, has reported that the academic work covered in an undergraduate degree at a leading UK institution provided him with little useful material to guide his work as a sport psychologist in Premiership football. Some of the possible reasons behind this situation have been discussed by Corlett (1996a), Ravizza (2002a) and Nesti (2004). These accounts and other valuable contributions, such as Gilbourne and Richardson's (2006) work about the importance of understanding culture in professional football, continue to be largely ignored by a sport psychology research community apparently more interested in publishing positivist research than in providing theoretically rich accounts of real-world practice. Until this is remedied, it will continue to be the case that often recently well qualified sport psychologists reject most of what they have been taught because it is perceived to be irrelevant to their work in professional sport and football. Having worked closely with a number of these individuals now operating in Premiership football and elite professional sports I frequently hear that there is a desire to pursue business-related qualifications such as MBAs, or to take courses in occupational psychology. Others wonder why they did not study counselling psychology in greater depth in their sport psychology or sport science degrees, which might have provided them with useful knowledge and skills to meet the needs of their current vocation.

DOING THE JOB

Given the fact that the playing staff at a professional football club change quite significantly from season to season, it is important to have some form of support to help new players to settle in to their new environment. In the Premiership, the rapid increase in the number of overseas players in most teams has added a new dimension to the work of a liaison officer. Many of these players will have little previous experience of England or English culture. This can extend to crucial factors relating to living arrangements, laws, and important cultural markers and traditions. When players bring their family with them the workload for the liaison officer is added to. The liaison officer can help find suitable accommodation for the player and his family, which can extend to guiding them about options connected to renting or buying a house,

126

and advice on finding an area suitable to their personal circumstances. For example, many players like to be close to the training ground and, if they have a family, then access to schools, health services and other local amenities can be very important.

At Premiership levels all these tasks are aimed at helping to create a culture of excellence to ensure that a player's domestic arrangements and personal circumstances do not become a contributing factor to poor performances. Although most players would be quite capable of planning and organizing these tasks, they can sometimes be rather involved, complex and may take a considerable period of time to deal with satisfactorily. Within Premiership football and other elite-level professional clubs, there is a belief that resources should be maximized where possible. This often means that it is necessary for players to have many of their external and domestic chores taken care of by someone else on their behalf; this is seen as a significant form of performance support.

It is important to highlight that clubs will invest in one or more liaison officers, or in some cases have this work carried out by external professional consultancies, because of their desire to ensure that new and existing players do not experience distractions that could interfere with playing and training. The overriding concern is to meet the needs of the players and to help create stability in their lives outside football, without being intrusive. This type of support should not be confused with lifestyle management. The service provided by liaison staff is usually more focused than this. Some of the very specific duties can include helping players to deal with financial matters relating to tax, invoices, purchasing items for their homes and dealing with banks. There are occasions where a player's agent may be able to provide this level of support, but often the liaison officer is in a much better position to offer such assistance, given that they are based in the club and know the city or area thoroughly. This local knowledge can be absolutely crucial in a number of other ways. Guidance on finding living accommodation in areas that allow good access to local shopping and other amenities can be particularly important for new and overseas players and their families. The liaison officer may be able to help players to select accommodation where they are more easily able to live relatively normal lives and feel that they can become integrated into their local communities should they wish this.

CARING OR PERFORMANCE FOCUSED

Two of the most important issues facing many players, especially those with young families, are schooling and health services. Liaison officers' extensive local contacts and in-depth knowledge means that they can be skilled at helping players and their families to meet these needs. In order to be effective, it is important to gain the trust of the player and their family. A dedicated liaison officer will have the time, skills and personal qualities to carry out this task. In order to identify needs correctly, it is essential that a close relationship exists between the player and the liaison staff. A potential danger in such a relationship could arise when a liaison officer spends more time with players they personally like rather than with those whose needs may be greater. Despite this, the ideal of a close relationship is of great importance for other key reasons. The first of these is that the liaison officer will often be the most knowledgeable of all the staff, including the manager, about any difficulties that a player is encountering in their broader lives. This information, where agreed upon with the player, can be usefully relayed to the manager or appropriate staff member, to assist the player and support them further if necessary. This is also helpful to the work of the sport psychologist. As has been discussed throughout this book, many of the most important psychological issues affecting performance of players relate to factors in their lives beyond the game. The liaison officer may be the first person at the club to know about some of these difficulties. Although confidentiality is absolutely central to be able to develop a good and trusting relationship with the player and players' families, there will be times when it is beneficial to the player for the liaison officer to mention the problems being faced. These may be contributing to poor attitudes in training, negative moods and a lack of focus in matches. These and many other facets relating to match and training performance could be affected. For example, if a player was very unhappy with their accommodation and felt isolated, lonely and frustrated, some of these feelings could impact negatively on their performance as a professional football player.

A further area in which the liaison officer can assist the sport psychologist is in providing a form of induction for a new player. Often a player, especially one from overseas, will have little knowledge of the area, traditions of the club and the culture of the people. This type of information is vitally important for them to understand the perceptions of local media and the club's fans.

It is often the case that a team and its fans see themselves as the guardians of a particular identity. For example, some clubs see themselves as custodians of the passing game, whilst for others the most important quality they have adopted relates to hard work and resilience. Although the relationship between clubs, their traditions and the history and culture of the town or city are complex and dynamic, the liaison officer can provide a useful service by inducting a player into this reality. This work can be done in conjunction with the sport psychologist. The sport psychologist working with a new player can carry out a further series of induction sessions, at which the player learns about team expectations, their role, codes of conduct and related matters. Within small, medium and large businesses and public sector organizations, induction is taken very seriously to ensure that the new employee can start their job in the best possible way. Until recently, most elite professional football clubs have tended to adopt a laissez-faire approach, assuming that players will eventually pick up ideas over time. There are two major potential problems with this approach. The player who is not shown the correct way and does not understand club expectations and operating practices may fall into bad habits out of ignorance rather than through deliberate actions. For example, a lack of knowledge about the degree of formality or informality that exists between senior players and youth players, expectations of timekeeping and commitment to community-based activities carried out on behalf of the club, and mechanisms to voice opinions to manager and other senior staff could cause uncomfortable moments (or worse!) for players early in their career with the club. The other useful reason for carrying out an induction is to allow the sport psychologist and liaison officer to demonstrate that the club is committed to a professional culture that attends to detail and offers a broad range of support to the player in order to maximize performance. The induction session with the liaison officer and psychologist could also address issues to do with media and responsibilities regarding public appearances. This may lead to directing the player to attend either 'in-house' or external courses to enhance their skills and confidence in dealing with the media.

The existence of liaison support services in Premiership clubs and elite professional football is further evidence that, unlike much of the literature in academic sport psychology (e.g. Andersen 2009) there is a strong belief that what happens in a player's life off the pitch is of crucial importance to their performance in matches and games. Clubs are very unlikely to pay for these services if they did not have evidence of cases where players have failed to perform, and sometimes have been sold or moved on, because they have been unable to settle into a new area or understand the expectations of the fans and local media.

In conclusion, it should be pointed out that this form of support is not about making sure that elite sports performers can have an easy life by avoiding taking responsibility for the ordinary day-to-day matters that 99 per cent of the population must deal with alongside performing successfully in their jobs or vocations. The clubs have not been guided by research in sport psychology; however, their approach is very much based on evidence-based practice. Their investment in staff to carry out liaison duties unambiguously demonstrates that clubs are convinced that caring for a sport performer's welfare is not just ethically sound but is vital to enhance performance.

The vignette that follows is based on a number of experiences that liaison staff frequently experience in their work at Premiership football clubs. The link between this and the work of the sport psychologist is a particular feature of this example. There are occasions where the liaison officer and sport psychologist must meet players together in order to help them to resolve a particular issue. More usually, the liaison officer will be able to help guide the sport psychologist's work with a player through informing him either about their general mood, motivation and other psychological matters and sometimes by discussing a specific issue in detail.

> Sport psychologist: 'How are you getting on with Dave at the moment? Has he settled in to that new house yet? The reason I'm asking is that for the past two to three weeks I have heard the staff complaining about his lack of focus in training and they don't appear confident to start him in the 11 at the moment.'
>
> Liaison officer: 'I meant to speak to you about him. Two nights ago

I went over to have a meal with him and his wife and to give them some help with some paperwork relating to the new house and trying to get some furniture in. I got the impression that not all is as good as it first appeared about the house. I think they have got "cold feet". It's just they didn't show any great enthusiasm for the tasks which I suppose is quite normal given it was quite boring paperwork in a language that they don't understand too well. It's just that when it came to choosing furniture and trying to get this ordered, I felt I was making all of the running.'

Sport psychologist: 'Do you think that it is about the house, or is it part of something bigger? Do you think he is happy here at the club, or is he wondering if he has made the wrong decision to have signed a three-year contract with us? It's just that the way we play and the expectations of our fans are so different from his last club. It must be tough coming to such a very different country compared to his home.'

Liaison officer: 'I don't think it's about that because he has only been here a short time and it is only natural that someone coming to something so strange would take a long time to get used to things.'

Sport psychologist: 'I would agree with you except this is someone who has a reputation for being a player who knows their own mind, what they can achieve, and what they need to do to succeed. Their record in three different countries at the highest level has been very good, and given this is someone in their early thirties, I am wondering why he is not settling in faster. He is playing in the same position and role that he had in his previous club, and the fitness staff and sports medicine staff say he is in excellent physical shape.'

Liaison officer: 'I think I need to take him out away from the city for a while when we have a break coming up. I know they both like the countryside and I think it would be good if I booked them into a hotel away from here for a break. Could be just a chance to get their thoughts back together and may be, to be able to "look up" for the first time for a while. After all, they have had a very hectic start to the season.'

This type of dialogue is commonplace between sport psychologists and liaison staff. The confidential nature of the work of both of these individuals in a professional football club means that players are often prepared to discuss a wide range of issues that they would be reluctant to express elsewhere. In many ways the relationship between a sport psychologist and a liaison officer is similar to that between the sport psychologist and the club chaplain. Questions about the details of issues, when something should be discussed in depth and where matters should be kept completely private are faced by many other individuals who work in the helping professions. For example, within professions associated with health and education, professional bodies provide guidelines to assist staff to operate confidentially and to ensure that client–practitioner trust is maintained. However, beyond written guidelines, there are practices and conventions relating to the sharing of information. Although this is usually addressed in detailed documentation, the standard requirement is that professionals must use their judgement in deciding what to share and how much should be divulged. This type of professional judgement extends to the work of sport psychologists and liaison officers operating in elite professional football. The overriding aim must be that whatever is discussed between the parties must be for the benefit of the client.

The liaison officer decided that having discussed a short trip out of the region with the player and his wife, he would visit them during their break and ask them about how things were really going for them since they had arrived at the club. What follows is an extract from a key part of this discussion.

> Liaison officer: 'If you are saying that maybe the house is not right for you then maybe we can still do something about it. It is in a desirable area with good schools and shops nearby and I'm sure it could easily be rented out if you would like this. We could then have a look at maybe renting an apartment out of the city in the other town you mentioned you would like to live in. Would you like me to have a look at some properties and get estate agents to suggest something that fits the bill?
>
> Dave (player): 'That would be really helpful. We would both like that because I don't think it's going to work where we are.'

Sarah (player's wife): 'I would like that much better because I feel that the house is absolutely great but the area is too quiet, and all of my new friends live a long way from where we are. I think maybe I fell in love with the house. In fact we both fell in love equally with the house. It's a pity one of us didn't have any reservations then we might not have done this. It's just maybe that because we will be here for three years, and it seemed such a fantastic price, that it seemed to make so much sense!'

Liaison officer: 'Ok, well I'm glad that I'm going to be about to help you with this and there is no point in staying in something that doesn't make you happy. It is too important for both of you and it can't be easy for Dave coming in to train and perform at his best in games when both of you are worried that you have made the wrong decision. This house will get rented within the month, absolutely no problem. If you remember, the estate agent said that they had people waiting to rent this property if you decided not to buy.'

Dave (player): 'The thing is and I haven't really told anyone yet but my wife is having a baby in five months' time. And we didn't want to keep living in the hotel. It's not easy in that situation and maybe that's another reason we moved on the house so quickly. I have not told the manager or any of the other staff and to be honest, between the house and the baby there has been quite a few things to deal with and even though I have played in this country for two years before and know a bit about its culture, Sarah had never been here and although her English is almost perfect, this is all so different and new. Both of us have been worrying a bit about when the baby arrives and not having family in this country and things like that.'

Liaison officer: 'Have you told the sport psychologist [George]? It's up to you of course but it's just that I know you have been working with him, and I'm sure he will have come across your type of situation plenty of times in the past. He tells me that there are more research studies on the sorts of things you are speaking about now but there's lots of really important psychological theory that can be useful in helping you to make sense of your situation and to choose the best thing for you at this moment. I think that maybe you should speak to him if you would like because you can speak in absolute confidence with him. I know he mentioned to me that your performance data and your own assessments on how you have been doing so far in the team are not as good as usual. I know he wondered if there was something either at the club, about your role in the team or maybe something in your outside lives that was affecting this.'

Dave: 'I should have told him but we've been trying to sort it out by kind of putting it to the back of our minds. I want to be a success here and Sarah has been very strong in supporting me in this. Just maybe I should acknowledge that I have asked a lot of her and ourselves this time. We have faced three big things at the same time; a new country and a new culture, a baby due, and buying a new house. Oh, and on top of that, new team-mates, new manager and identity of the club that I am still learning about! I suppose our few days here in the hills at this hotel have been a chance to try and begin to get these things clear in our minds.'

Sarah: 'I have been really pleased for Dave to speak to the sport psychologist so that you, Simon [liaison officer], can tell him a bit about our circumstances and that as soon as we're all back in training, that Dave would really like to have a chat with him. I know early in his career he worked with a sport psychologist in [country x] and they didn't seem to think that what went on outside of the training complex or football itself had much bearing on things! I remember being amazed that they didn't understand that sometimes his concentration and focusing problems were not to do with football itself, but related to the fact that his father and brother had both been made redundant from their jobs, and that as a result there was lots of difficulties in their very close family. I remember the psychologist saying they were a sport psychologist and that meant they were experts in sports and performance. I often wondered afterwards if that person had maintained that view given how many athletes they must now have worked with who have difficult times with their performances because of things outside of their sport. Don't get me wrong, Dave was not in need of medical [i.e. clinical psychology] support, as he was fine, but he did have some tough things to deal with. Maybe she [i.e. the sport psychologist] only thought of Dave as *just* as a footballer instead of a *person*!'

EDUCATION AND WELFARE OFFICERS

Instead of liaison officers, education and welfare officers are often employed by clubs at academy and youth levels. Their role is to help young players maintain some involvement in their education and to assist them with life outside football.

This may mean that they manage their educational experience by ensuring that players attend to their studies. It could also mean providing guidance on which courses and awards to pursue, and giving career guidance in case they do not become professionals. Through this support the officer can encourage the young players to learn more about sport psychology and sport science to assist their knowledge and own preparation for performance. The close and frequent contact means that the education and welfare officer can become a form of mentor for the players. Usually not part of the academy coaching staff, although viewed as a key member of staff, the pastoral support element of this job is vitally important.

These individuals may also work closely with the sport psychologist on issues like dealing with unhelpful parents, homesickness, relationship problems and confidence issues. These and other experiences can affect many of the young players, making them feel angry, unhappy or unsuccessful. In many ways this is similar to the work of the liaison officer in that trust and confidentiality are essential.

The education and welfare officer may refer a young player to the sport psychologist to help deal with these types of issues and topics. This can also work well where the sport psychologist can seek the advice or guidance from the education and welfare officer to assist the choices of a young player. The staff in these clubs are often excellent allies for the sport psychologist because of a shared background in education and a concern with growth and development of the whole person.

The sport psychologist will be able to work alongside the education and welfare officer in delivering group and small unit sessions. These could address issues such as the importance of young players maintaining a disciplined approach to their personal and social life. It is easy to see how these topics and other similar examples are equally about personal welfare, future development and performance in the sport. This is another key area where practice at the highest levels of sport challenges those restricted views held by some in sport psychology. Put in blunt terms, clubs would not invest millions of pounds in this type of support throughout the Premiership if they did not have sound evidence that caring for young players' development off the pitch is a major factor in their success on it.

7

TRUST, VALUES, CONFIDENTIALITY AND IDENTITY

TRUST

Professional footballers and youth players hoping to make the grade at professional clubs (Parker 2001) will inevitably encounter many of the following experiences over their careers: being dropped from the starting line up or first team squad; suffering injury and loss of form; being sent out on loan or sold to another club; and being lauded one week and vilified the next, by the media, supporters and other stakeholders. These experiences place great demands on the mental skills and psychological qualities of players. They also remind individuals that gaining someone's trust in them can sometimes be a long and tortuous process. Trust is a commonly used term in professional football. It extends from trust between players on the field of play, to the trust that managers have in their staff and players, and trust players have in their support staff, including the sport psychologist.

Without a high level of confidence and self-belief, coupled with a significant amount of self- or intrinsic motivation and trust in themselves, players will struggle and most likely fail to have a long and successful career at the highest level. Whilst skills associated with developing better concentration, focus and interpreting feedback constructively can all be taught and acquired, these will not be sufficient for players to withstand the pressure-cooker environment that exists in this sport at such elevated levels of performance. There will be many occasions where players will need to rely on deeper and more personal aspects of their character in order to deal positively with the difficult moments and the great successes that come their way. The capacity to achieve this depends to a significant degree on how much they are willing to trust in their talents and are prepared to follow their own assessments and goals, especially when their ability and performances are being questioned (i.e. distrusted) by others.

For players to be able to develop trust in themselves, to allow them to take on the many exciting and tough challenges in professional football, is of major importance. Research to date has offered much on motivation, confidence and other psychological skills in elite-level sport (Williams 2006). Surprisingly, there are very few references to trust in the sport psychology literature. Future studies should turn their attention to examining why trust is mentioned so readily in professional sport, what this refers to and how it can be developed.

From a professional practice perspective, trust has been a key applied value in my work in professional football. Gaining the trust of the manager, players and senior staff in the role of a sport psychologist involves a number of factors: being able to meet the needs of those you are working with; becoming part of the team; being able to explain your role accurately to different audiences or clients; displaying integrity; being able to pursue clear goals; demonstrating an in-depth understanding of the culture and its practices; and finally, being able to maintain complete confidentiality at all times. All these factors are of crucial importance, and sport psychologists will constantly work to achieve these during their time with a club or consultancy.

However, confidentiality differs from other items in the list in that it must be met fully by the sport psychologist from first to last.

TRUSTING YOURSELF

In terms of the difficulties that players frequently encounter, one of the most challenging relates to being dropped from the team or squad. It is often the case that the real reasons behind this are little known by the players themselves, although not infrequently the media and supporters of the team will often assume that they know why such action has taken place. The culture within most Premiership football clubs and elite professional sports organizations is one where privacy is jealously guarded.

This distrust of outsiders is understandable given the huge national and international interest in the sport, and the decisions that are made about players and teams. A further reason for the concern with confidentiality and privacy is to do with the competitive structure of the Premier League. Quite simply, clubs do not want their inner workings, especially where these involve real or perceived disputes with players, to provide an advantage to their opponents. In circumstances such as these, Premiership players often have to keep their own counsel, despite misunderstandings and misinformation surrounding their situation. To be able to demonstrate this level of control and composure, whilst still working hard to get back into the team, places a very considerable demand on individual players.

The sport psychologist working within the club, or as a consultant engaged externally, can be extremely useful at such times. These critical moments (Nesti and Littlewood 2009) occur frequently in the careers of top-level sports performers, and, although very difficult to deal with, they do provide an opportunity for players and sports performers to develop greater self-knowledge and a number of important qualities. One of the most helpful psychological qualities at moments like this is the ability to trust your own self-image rather than being distracted by the image constructed by others. In top-level professional football these others can include the manager, local and national media, fans and – for Premiership players – even the general public and politicians.

A sport psychologist working with a player during this period may find much to their surprise that their sessions focus as much on the values held by the player as on psychological strategies and techniques. For example, the importance of acting in a professional fashion and continuing to do the job required to the best of their ability is something that is only possible where players adopt a courageous stance to the situation they are confronting. This type of courage involves a player in working hard quietly to do the right things, despite being ignored and even abused by senior staff at the club, supporters and the media. To be able to withstand such an uncomfortable and anxiety-inducing phase, the sport psychologist may able to help the player to reflect more deeply on what they stand for and who they believe themselves to be (i.e. their self-image).

Despite sounding rather abstract and philosophical, these factors can often turn out to be crucial in helping players to maintain their best work and follow their professional responsibilities, no matter how well these are received within the club or the broader environment.

Some players I have worked with in Premier League football and from other levels of professional football have described how they have had to think carefully about what their core values are in order to find a deeper reason to continue fighting for their place and when dealing with often very harsh and brutal experiences in the game. Given the particular traditions associated with the culture of professional football in the UK (see Chapter 1), players can sometimes find themselves ostracized, and treated as though they no longer exist. Whilst some players have been conditioned through many years to accept this dysfunctional behaviour as the norm, there are others from different cultures, or with different personality types and experiences, who are not prepared to accept these types of bullying behaviours.

For these individuals the sport psychologist can provide a useful form of support through formal and informal mechanisms. This may involve brief conversations where the player talks about the important driving forces that keep him motivated to do the best he can in ugly circumstances. The words used here will relate to honesty, integrity, values and making sure they are true to themselves.

According to one of the most important writers on existential psychology, being yourself is something that eludes most people, most of the time (Kierkegaard 1944 [1844]). In contrast, authenticity has been defined by existential psychologists as involving placing trust in your values and trying to live by these, *despite the difficulties this may cause the person.*

Being authentic and able to trust one's own judgements is considered to be crucial to assist an individual to maintain a sound performance focus irrespective of the situation they face (Nesti 2004). Players frequently talk about being able to 'look at themselves in the mirror'. By this expression they mean that they are able to recognize the importance of self-acceptance. Self-acceptance is also strongly related to the idea of trust.

The issue of values can also arise during more formal sessions with players. This may be because a player has been having a difficult time at the club, involved in a breakdown in communication with the manager and other key staff, or because they are struggling to deal with new expectations placed upon them. Sometimes the critical moments facing a player can arise because of excellent performances. In these situations and phases, it may be that the player is feeling anxious about the new demands and levels that are required, and lack the confidence to sustain this consistently over time. When players perform exceptionally well they sometimes begin to put additional pressure on themselves and start to set new and unrealistic goals. In meeting the player during these moments the sport psychologist may be able to assist through dialogue about goals. Sometimes though, it may be deeper than this. The setting of inappropriate goals may be more to do with the players having temporarily pulled away from the important values that have sustained them in their progress in the game. This can sometimes turn into a discussion of identity.

At times players may spend time looking back at their career to date and discussing how they managed to deal with new expectations and success at different points of their journey. Players mention that the quality of humility, staying grounded, remembering who they are, and more importantly where they have come from, are important factors in helping them to successfully negotiate this particular challenge.

The player and sport psychologist may find themselves discussing the key moments that are etched in the memory of the player that relate to how they were able to meet the new demands associated with increased success. In some ways, it appears to be a paradox; great success has been accompanied by an increased recognition that their deepest-held values have sometimes been the most important anchors during these experiences. Recognition that success has been achieved because of luck, hard work, ability and being courageous enough to choose the right decisions helps players to feel pride in their accomplishments, whilst also keeping them humble. In my dealings with Premiership players and other elite sports performers, I have been impressed by how often the most high-achieving and successful performers are those who have still retained a large amount of humility.

This topic has rarely been addressed in the sport psychology literature, although Crust (2007) has suggested that this quality may be part of mental toughness. The general neglect of humility is extremely unfortunate, given that anecdotal accounts, reports based on interviews with top managers and performers in world sport, and the ideas of some of the greatest philosophers and thinkers such as Socrates, Aquinas and Pascal have emphasized how crucial this value is. Humility has been discussed in relation to sound ethical behaviour, morality and spirituality in sport (Robinson 2007); however, there is a lack of research or scholarly work relating to the importance of this term for sport performance in general and professional football in particular.

IDENTITY AND TRUST

One of the most important aspects of a high-performing team centres on the concept of identity. The team identity is ultimately based on the values espoused by the individuals within the team and the collective unit itself. This is something much discussed in professional football and is of great concern to elite sports organizations and teams. Unfortunately, there is a paucity of literature in sport psychology that deals with identity and the team in a suitably in-depth and real way.

The sport psychologist has an excellent opportunity to assist with the development of a team identity. Identity can be considered on a number of different levels. An identity of a team is made up of the identities of each member; however, where these are in conflict team identity can be weak and fractured. The major task facing the sport psychologist is to find an appropriate mechanism to encourage players and staff to think about the relationship between team identity and performance. Within a professional sports environment, the overriding concern is with results. The identity of the team must be one that assists the unit to achieve more positive results. Identity therefore should not be viewed as something abstract, purely philosophical or an attractive set of slogans that can be used only in marketing.

142

Although there is little empirical literature on this topic, there are some examples in the literature of where identity has been highlighted as being important to individual athletes. Balague (1999) has discussed this concept in relation to meaning in sport and Brewer *et al.* (1993) have studied athletic identity and self-identity in retirement and career transition in sport. Psychological research on transitions, identity and performance in professional football are urgently required to understand more about how this important issue affects the lives of young players and those in the first team environment.

The identity of a professional football team can often evolve and emerge clearly over time. This can reflect the achievements of the team, the personality of team members and also the values and identity of the manager in particular. It could be argued that this may be the most effective and authentic way for a team identity to be formed. However, this can take a considerable period time to happen, and not all members of the team may understand its identity in the same way. Conflicting views of identity can be very destructive in this type of environment. If the manager and staff wish the team to possess one type of identity, and players and supporters would rather see something different, there is much room for misunderstanding and conflict. The optimum situation is where there is congruence between players, supporters and the staff in relation to the current identity of the team and where the team identity should develop in the future.

CREATING IDENTITY

Particularly in teams where there has been a significant change in playing personnel, there is an opportunity for the sport psychologist, with the support of the manager, to carry out team-based sessions focusing on the issue of identity. This can allow new players to quickly understand how the team and club they have recently joined views itself. This is not a superficial exercise in creating labels or managing brands. The identity of a team is based on the goals and wishes of the club as a whole. It is also, in a more profound sense, based on the dominant values of the group. In professional football it is no exaggeration to say that the values of the players, the manager (including to some extent their staff) and even the club itself are most visibly expressed through the team's identity.

One of the ways that team identity can be built upon and clarified is through small unit exercises. The sport psychologist can give the players an extensive list of words or phrases and ask them to select three or four that most closely capture the current identity of the team. A similar exercise could be done in relation to aspirations concerning future team identity. Given the multicultural nature of most Premiership clubs, the sport psychologist may need to have words translated into several different languages to ensure all team members are able to contribute equally. Discussions can then take place on the merits of particular words or phrases, to enable the selection of three or four, which can be then be used in descriptions of the team's identity. These words can then be included on presentation slides, reports to players, pre-match analysis presentations, and on any other documents that players receive within the club.

This small gesture can have a powerful effect in reminding players and staff of what they would like their team to be described as. For example, a list of words could include terms frequently associated with high-performing teams in sport, and non-sport domains. Being competitive, winners, honest, hard-working, imaginative, inventive, spirited, tenacious and other similar evocative terms can be presented to the players. It is also possible and desirable that the team or groups of players suggest their own additional words or phrases that they consider best describe the team identity.

The value of this type of exercise is that it can also be particularly useful when the team faces difficult moments. The existence of familiar words around team identity can allow the sport psychologist, with the support of other key staff, to remind players about how important these terms are. This could involve players working in small groups to enhance engagement by looking more closely at what these terms mean in practice. Discussions about the word competitive may help players to understand that this is something that draws on both physical and psychological elements. This could be described in terms of the need to ensure that preparation for training and not just matches is carried out with appropriate intensity and dedication to ensure that each session

144

is characterized by players giving their all to succeed. Consideration on this word could also lead to an important debate about the importance of remaining competitive in matches against teams where there is little expectation of a positive result. If coaching staff are involved in these discussions, there may be dialogue about very specific tactical and physical requirements that are essential to fulfil a competitive identity.

Using this approach makes it more likely that the team subscribes to a set of words that really represent their collective values. For example, in sports like professional Rugby League, honesty is an important and frequently used term. This refers to much more than trying to do your job well and accepting responsibilities for your errors and failings. In fact, this word is identified by coaches at the highest level of the sport as best representing the most important values they expect to see in their players and teams. Honesty in this context means being prepared to be selfless, sacrifice yourself for the greater good of the team, accept responsibility for your actions, and never to shirk a challenge. This account of honesty supports the view of those psychologists (Gilbourne and Richardson 2006) who contend that psychological skills, personal qualities and values are inextricably linked (of course, this should not be understood as saying that these *all mean the same thing*).

Beyond exercises with the players the sport psychologist may wish to involve the staff and the manager in discussions about current team identity. This will allow them to examine the different views that may exist between them in relation to player perceptions. This could allow both staff and players to have important information on each others' views about the current team identity, which could reveal a high degree of similar understanding or may suggest that there are important differences between the two groups. This staff may choose not to share this information with the players, or they may spend time discussing it with them. Either way, it is likely to be extremely useful information for the staff and manager, especially in terms of developing team identity in the future.

The sport psychologist may be able to carry out small group and individual sessions with the staff to gather information on where they would like the team identity to develop in the future. This can present an opportunity for a closer examination and in-depth analysis of what processes and practices will need to be put in place to generate the preferred future identity. The staff will be able to suggest how their own work can formally and informally begin to assist this to take place. Quite clearly the coaches and sports science staff who work on a daily basis with the players, individually and collectively, have a great deal of influence over this process.

Where words like inventiveness or imagination have been chosen as part of a team identity, there will need to be a scouting and recruitment policy that aims to attract players with these technical skills and psychological and personal qualities. The team identity also has implications for training methods, processes around communication and the level of responsibility given to players. Becoming a team capable of moments of great invention in match play is not something that is the responsibility of one or two individuals. The culture must help facilitate this aspect of a team's identity, which will need to be one where players are encouraged to be creative, take risks and support each other in these tasks. This may take a considerable time to achieve. The sport psychologist can play an important part in this by reminding players and staff that these changes do not happen easily or quickly, and that they are facilitated by both informal and spontaneous actions as much as by more planned and systematic processes.

In terms of ensuring that tenacity or resilience is a key part of a team's identity, the sport psychologist can work closely with the performance analysts to show DVD footage and statistical data that reveals where the team has stuck to the game plan in difficult circumstances. The players and the staff will need to work hard to ensure the idea of tenacity is converted into a visible reality. It requires the ability to trust in the long-term goals that have been agreed, no matter how difficult the short-term situation may be.

INCULCATING THE VALUES OF EXCELLENCE

Staff at a professional football club have a very important role to play in terms of impacting on the underlying values which players are expected to adhere to. The dominant values operating across the staff will have an effect on their job satisfaction, effectiveness and ability to deal with the

146

rapid fluctuations in fortune that are increasingly experienced within elite-level professional sport. Individual staff members will bring their own values and ethics to the group. Despite this, staff team harmony and success is much more likely to occur where there are shared values and where these values are sound and ethical.

The importance of values and their relationship to achievement in organizations have received much attention in recent years in the world of business. Major companies and organizations are increasingly aware of how important it is to customers and the broader public to be associated with ethical values. In addition, there is a growing recognition that staff motivation and morale is directly linked to the types of values that operate within an organization. Some of the world's most successful and well-established commercial organizations learned these lessons many years ago. It is recognized that companies like Marks & Spencer have long seen the benefits of treating their staff as the most important resource within their organization; this can be seen through their recruitment, training and development policies, and how these companies respect the human needs of their staff and those of the local community.

Within a Premiership football club or other professional sports environment, the same rule applies. The sport psychologist can draw on the importance of sound values that exist in some of the most successful non-sport organizations to demonstrate how important this dimension is in terms of both ethical practice and performance enhancement. This does not mean there is a need for prolonged and in-depth academic discussions on the importance of values such as honesty, trust and integrity. However, there are ways in which these and other important values can be sustained or engendered within the team. One of the ways to address this within a Premiership club could be through one-to-one and small group meetings with staff at which the sport psychologist seeks to highlight the difference between short-term strategies and longer-term success. The tempo and rhythm of high-level professional sport means that very often individuals and staff teams are forced to adopt a pragmatic and even cynical approach to decisions and processes. There is a recognition from most at an individual and group level that this is not always a constructive way to operate.

In order to pursue long-term goals and to attempt to make changes that will not have an impact immediately there needs to be agreement about why it is worthwhile to plan for the future. This issue can be addressed by getting the staff to examine what type of organization they would like to be a part of. This is first of all about requiring staff to accept that they do have some control over their own futures and that it is beneficial and motivating to think about this. At this stage, dialogue may be centred on specific topics, such as the relationship between youth development and the first team, the future identity of a club, or changes to players recruitment policy. All these factors are influenced by finance and whether there is a realistic opportunity and a desire to grow the club in a particular direction. At a deeper level, commitment to these and other initiatives will undoubtedly test the values held by the club, the individuals operating at boardroom level and the coaching and backroom staff. This latter group can be powerful advocates for change, speaking as they do with an intimate and close knowledge of the performance end of the business. The sport psychologist will be able to help with the generation of agreed team values that will provide the necessary ballast when circumstances threaten future plans.

THREAT TO VALUES

The alternative to the holding of common values within the staff team is where there is radically differing or substantially competing views about what is important and why things should be done in a particular way. When this is the situation at a club, there tends to be a breakdown in communication between individuals and departments, and often a lack of professional respect rises to the surface. The club may now have a staff team who appear socially cohesive at a surface level, but are driven by a very different set of values and beliefs about ethical and professional practice. The sport psychologist must attempt to overcome such a fracture within the staff team. In this task the support of the manager and other well-respected and experienced staff is paramount.

The mechanisms through which this can be addressed are many and varied, including use of external consultants, especially those with experience of this scenario in equally fast-moving and pressurized

148

business environments. The sport psychologist could also use confidential one-to-ones with individuals whose stated values differ substantially from those held by other members of the staff team. Sometimes it may be more appropriate to address this issue in small groups or even through meetings of the whole staff team. In individual meetings little will be achieved unless the member of staff believes that he can express his views in complete confidence. This is unlikely to take place if the member of staff does not trust the sport psychologist because of a poor working relationship between them, or does not agree about values and beliefs. This suggests that confidentiality is not just something that must be offered by a sport psychologist but is something that depends on the client's trust in the psychologist and the psychologist's integrity.

Other ways of beginning to deal with such a potentially damaging rupture can be determined by the sport psychologist according to the operational context and environment. It may be possible to speak out at group meetings about common values and seek support for these from the rest of the staff. The sport psychologist would be expected to lead discussions on values since they are central to team cohesion, identity, communication, long-term goals and other related issues that the psychologist has been employed to deal with. Although the topic of values does not require a philosophical discussion for there to be recognition of their importance to everyday practice and future policy in a professional football club, on occasions the sport psychologist may decide to talk about the need to confront failings in this area. This must be done as diplomatically as possible given that most people are defensive when challenged about their values, since, as Salter (1997) has argued, values are in many ways the most important part of an individual's personality and identity.

Despite this, there will be inevitable moments where the sport psychologist is likely to be the lone voice in directing the staff to consider their values and the implications of these for the situations facing the club and team. The most important and difficult period to stress the importance of values will be where teams find themselves in and around the relegation zone, or experiencing repeated failures. To be able to ask questions about values, and whether the staff team are applying the agreed team values consistently, could be a highly uncomfortable experience for the sport psychologist. Because of the extremely close working relationship that exists in most staff teams in elite professional sport, any questioning about important and fundamental issues like values can easily be mistaken for unfair and harsh criticism. The sport psychologist will need to approach these occasions with some degree of caution.

This, however, must not prevent them from speaking the candid word. The intention at these moments must be clear for all staff members to see. Discussions about whether the staff are staying true to their values may be hard to carry out. It is possible though that the team will understand why the sport psychologist must ask these questions, especially during difficult times, since this is one of the key reasons that the club employs them in the first place.

The passion and motivation that exists within the staff can sometimes lead to a closing up or breakdown in intergroup communication. On these occasions, the sport psychologist may decide that it is right to ask staff if the failure to communicate with players or other staff members is consistent with the specific professional values they aspire to. When professional and elite-level sports teams, including those in Premiership football, talk about honesty and courage, these values usually extend to ensuring that there is unambiguous, transparent and constructive communication between the parties at all times.

These values are most likely to be tested during those inevitable moments of crisis, when teams are performing poorly, when results are not going as hoped and when staff fear for their jobs. The values of courage and integrity are vividly seen during these moments. Courage, which Aquinas suggests is something opposed to self-interest, is by definition required only in difficult situations or when facing arduous events (Corlett 1996b). Integrity may be defined as the capacity to stay true to ones values despite pressures and temptations to abandon these, at least temporarily. It is clear from these accounts that both courage and integrity in the final analysis can only be acquired by the individual. Their benefits, however, can extend to the group or the team.

The sport psychologist working in professional football does not need to provide lengthy and detailed accounts that explain definitions of courage and integrity. Their task is to respectfully, but clearly and without obfuscation, highlight the benefits that accrue to the team

150

where behaviours and practices are consistently based in these values. Although no empirical work has been carried out explicitly assessing the importance of values such as honesty, trust, integrity and courage in high-level professional football teams, experienced practitioners and anecdotal accounts attest to the fact that these are central to the identity of some of the most highly achieving clubs in the sport.

THE IMPORTANCE OF LIVING YOUR VALUES

In order to assist discussions with others about the importance of values and ethical practice, it is essential that sport psychologists are sure about their own position with regard to these. There is little time within an elite sports organization to begin to work out what values are central to how you intend to operate and what will be necessary to try to follow these as closely as possible. This has been described within a Premiership football club by Simon Hartley, a BASES accredited sport psychologist, who operated as a full-time member of the first team staff delivering fitness testing and psychological support in the 2001/02 season. Nesti (2004) has written an account of supervising this neophyte practitioner during his first season in Premiership football.

This highlights how important values are to professional practice, especially for relatively inexperienced sport psychologists. The chapter points out that sport psychologists at the club found that their values proved to be the most important factor in enabling them to provide a professional and effective support service for players and staff. This was described as being a considerable surprise to them, given that they anticipated that the delivery of mental skills training and team-based sessions on motivation, competitive anxiety and performance would be their most important tasks during the season.

Understanding why one is prepared to continue to offer a particular type of support, or suggest specific strategies to help the team or individuals during critical moments, ultimately rests on the values that underpin the sport psychologist's professional practice. The importance of ensuring congruence between professional practice and philosophy and values has been alluded to by Lindsay et al. (2007). Although their work does not address professional football, many sport psychologists who have worked within the Premier League and other football clubs would most likely be able to recognize the arguments made.

The importance of staying true to one's values in relation to practice cannot be underestimated, especially when what is offered might not always be welcomed or fully accepted. Ideally, sport psychologists should attempt to reflect on their values before commencing any work. They should be able to articulate why these values are considered essential to the ethical practice of their professional duties. One of the best ways to address this is for sport psychologists to engage in extensive reading on philosophy and ethics.

Articles and books written in accessible language that avoids many of the technical terminology of academic philosophy can be very useful. Literature by Pieper (1989) dealing with the concepts of courage, hope and trust is relatively easy to digest and yet contains an in-depth analysis rarely covered by most psychologists. A notable exception to this is the work of May (1975), which provides a psychological analysis of courage and creativity. Unfortunately, there is almost nothing of note on these concepts in the sport psychology literature, despite both terms being so often heard in Premiership and professional football, especially when managers are talking about the most important qualities they look for in their teams.

EQUALITY AND VALUES

One of the most important requirements that should govern the work of a sport psychologist is the need to work with everyone, irrespective of the situation in which the players find themselves. This is often much easier said than done. Players will be reluctant to work with sport psychologists during difficult phases unless they are certain that meetings will be completely confidential. Confidentiality is vital to develop trust so that players are prepared to speak openly and honestly about the situation they are in.

A Premiership football club usually contains a large squad of motivated and high-achieving players. These individuals are used to playing regularly, or at least being part of the squad for games. During a season there can be conflict and bad feeling between players and the manager or their senior staff, as a result of not being selected for the team. It is important to remember that a prolonged absence from match play can impact negatively on a player's fitness levels and undermine confidence, self-belief and motivation. This can result in a frustrated and despondent individual who may not train as well as he could. Such a situation can lead to the player having a negative attitude towards his work. This in turn can impact on the player's attitude to the training ground, and can heighten tensions between players, and between the player and the senior staff and manager.

The fluctuating nature of form, confidence and results will almost always mean that there will be significant changes to the playing squad and starting line-up over a season. This can happen very rapidly where players are suspended, injured or dropped because of a tactical necessity to set the team up in a different way. Sport psychologists in these situations must closely examine their professional practice values and ethical codes of conduct. Questions concerning the nature of the client may be particularly pertinent at this point. This issue has been discussed extensively in the sport psychology literature (Andersen 2005).

The answers to these ethical and professional practice dilemmas are fraught with difficulties. However, it is clear from the ethical codes of practice associated with BASES, the BPS Division of Sport and Exercise Psychology and other professional bodies that sport psychologists have a duty of care to carry out their work in a consistent and professional way. Where they have been appointed by a Premiership club or professional football team to work with players in group, small unit or individual sessions, they must do all that they reasonably can to fulfil this obligation. This means that confidentiality must be protected for the individual player first and, most importantly, not to do this properly will lead to unethical and unprofessional behaviour on the part of the psychologist and could destroy the trust that is so essential to doing work with professional athletes in such a publicly sensitized environment as Premiership football.

MEETING THE PERSON NOT THE PLAYER!

The following semi-fictional vignette looks at how professional practice values should govern the behaviour of sport psychologists in these frequently experienced and very demanding situations.

As I walked in to the training ground through the reception, I asked the security staff if they had seen Simon this morning. Simon was one of our new players that we had bought in the January transfer window from a top Championship club. To my surprise, the staff replied that they had just seen his two closest friends amongst the players, but that, unusually, he had not arrived with them at the same time. Simon was an affable and modest individual. In some ways he seemed very different from the stereotypes held by many people about top-level sports performers.

Maybe because he came from Africa and had played in Europe since being a very young man, he had acquired a depth of personality that was not always seen in his contemporaries, especially those from the UK. He was unafraid to talk about world affairs and politics, and read a lot about the economic and financial difficulties that impacted on his home country and beyond. Quietly spoken, but with a very determined air about him, Simon had great presence which was undoubtedly helped by his impressive physical stature.

I thought little of this initially, until I walked past the coaches' room. One of the coaching team asked me if I had had any one-to-one meetings in the past few days with Simon. Although this was quite a normal question, there was something different in how it was asked. I went into my office and sat down at the desk and began to listen to the messages that had been left on my mobile phone. I noticed a text message had been sent the evening before from Simon, apologizing for being unable to meet today for our planned one-to-one meeting at the stadium. This was a more lengthy session and was something that I usually organized with those players who were most in need of support, or who were receptive to sport psychology work. As the morning progressed it became clear that the manager had had a conversation with Simon at the end of training the day before. The coaching and fitness staff did not know the details of this conversation but when I asked about Simon's mood they confirmed that he seemed very down and unhappy.

Later that morning in the dining room where I usually grabbed a coffee as the players began to assemble before training, I noticed that Simon was sitting quietly apart from the group on his own, reading a magazine. Although he was rarely the centre of attention and liked to keep himself to himself, there appeared to be rather a different atmosphere from normal. Just at this point, the manager came walking through the dining room on his way to see a member of staff whose office was at the far end. I happened to glance over at a group of players including Simon at this point. There was a look on Simon's face that I had seen before in other players in these situations. The thought passed my mind that the conversation yesterday with the manager had been about something very important for the player, and that it had not gone particularly well.

Some minutes later the manager popped into my office and briefly mentioned that he did not want me to have any meetings with Simon, and to avoid informal dialogue with him where this was possible. We did not have an opportunity for a prolonged discussion about this, although he said that without a change in the player's attitude and mentality he would never feature in the first team again at this club.

As the manager left I was somewhat taken aback, since I knew that Simon was someone who wanted to succeed at this new level of football and was deeply committed to doing what was necessary to allow this to happen. In our sessions we had discussed his goals for the season and he had looked at all aspects of himself, both football-related and in his broader life in an effort to make it more likely that he could achieve in his new club. Our sessions were usually intense and there was a level of honesty and authenticity about the communication between us that usually left me feeling positive about our work together. During the last two meetings Simon had been wrestling with an attempt to understand why he was not making the inroads into the team that he had hoped for.

However, he had not been demoralized about this and spent much time discussing this difficult phase of his professional life in relation to other challenging moments that he had successfully overcome in his life beyond football. These led to an examination of what qualities and psychological skills he had developed as a result of passing successfully through these arduous moments, providing powerful accounts that I would summarize in writing and give to Simon as part of the confidential follow-up to our meetings.

Now it seemed that I would be unable to maintain lines of communication with him since the manager wanted him to be cut off from the group until he could see a change in attitude. I knew that this presented me with a dilemma that I had often experienced in my work with elite professional sports teams before. Although sometimes there is less clarity about how much time, if any, should be devoted to work with certain individuals, I often had to confront the issue of deciding whether to maintain my contact with players when senior staff in particular were either explicitly, or more usually, in more subtle implicit ways, indicating that they did not want the player to benefit from this type of support.

In other words, it is very common in the culture of some elite professional sports clubs and Premiership football for players to be ignored by the staff and attempts are made to cut them off from the group when their behaviour and attitudes are seen as disruptive, unprofessional or unsatisfactory. In Simon's case I knew that he was not being accused of the former two crimes but that it was the latter that had finally brought the manager to this decision.

Later that day as the players were leaving the training ground I deliberately watched them getting into their cars in the parking area to attempt to intercept Simon before he left. Again, in my experience, when a player is shunned and no longer feels part of the group it is important to do all that you can not to draw unnecessary attention to this in a public way. Players usually left the changing rooms after training in ones and twos rather than as large groups, and therefore it was an ideal opportunity to make contact in a relatively private and low-key way.

As Simon got into his car I wandered across in a fairly casual fashion and leaned against the front passenger door. A slight drizzle had begun, so Simon opened the passenger door and I sat down beside him. After a few words about the bitter winter weather and how he was feeling in terms of fitness, we had the following discussion:

'Did the manager call you in Simon, today, before you went out to train, as I heard that you met with him yesterday after training. How did that go?' I asked.

'Not good at all. I've come here excited and really motivated to get into the team and be a part of this, but for some reason I am getting further away each day. No one really tells me exactly what they want me to change or do, and I think that they feel they have made a mistake bringing me into the club,' Simon said.

'Why do you say that, Simon?' I began, 'You know that we spent months attempting to set up our recruitment of you. The staff team were so enthusiastic and delighted when it was confirmed that you were joining us this year. How has this happened?'

Simon looked down at nothing in particular, and fiddled about with his mobile phone in his hand. After a long pause he said, 'I am trying my best but I have never had anyone sit down and take real time to say exactly where I am doing well, and where they've got real concerns. How can someone expect me to pick up on things and change if they never tell me what those things are. I'll tell you something, when people don't tell you what they want from you, in my book it means that they maybe don't know, or that they don't respect me enough to have that kind of conversation.'

We continued talking for the next ten minutes or so, during which Simon expressed how frustrated and angry he was at how he was being treated. He knew that the manager and some of the staff were attempting to ignore him as some kind of punishment to get him to change. He asked whether I thought this was sound from an ethical and psychological perspective. The end of our brief session captured this in a powerful and succinct sentence. Simon said, 'I think that they will regret this way of behaving really soon because the games that are coming up away from home against [sides X] and [side Y], they will need me to play because the team tactics will have to change if we are to get anything out of those games.

'I have seen this before in other places but I'm really surprised to be experiencing this in Premiership football. I suppose it just goes to show that the massive pressure we are operating under that causes people to swing from the extremes of describing you in amazingly positive terms one minute, and then treating you as a non-person soon after. Whatever else that is, it is not how I think people should be treated. To be honest it is deeply disrespectful and does not help anyone in the long term. I think that as our sport psychologist, you need to let them know this is how some of us feel!'

I finished the session from my perspective by saying that I did raise this issue on different occasions with staff and the manager and that whilst some could see the validity in what I was saying, the overall view was that sport psychologists were unable to fully understand the world of elite professional sport and professional football in particular. This often seemed to turn into a debate with no satisfactory outcome, and where very experienced and highly capable staff were in effect seriously questioning the validity of the sport psychology 'mantra' about positive feedback and sound communication.

I finished by assuring Simon that, without breaking confidentiality, I would continue to express my professional opinion based on my professional ethics and codes of practice and values of honesty and personal integrity, and belief that, although punishments were a legitimate tool to use, these should not involve anything that looked like coercion, bullying or could lead to a complete breakdown in two-way communication. Simon looked over at me properly for the first time in our session that day, and gave a wistful smile: 'All the very best with that task, Mark. Good luck, and don't get yourself sacked!'

This vignette is intended to capture some of the difficult issues that sport psychologists will frequently encounter concerning values, confidentiality and trust in their work in professional team sport. I had decided to maintain a level of dialogue with the player despite being informed that I should not be working with him. The reality facing the sport psychologist on these occasions is that they must decide who their client is and be governed by how they will satisfy their professional and ethical practice as a sport psychologist in each situation they encounter. It is impossible to identify precisely what course of action should be taken in each and every case. Much will depend on the relationship between the sport psychologist, manager and other key staff, and the level of trust and confidence that they have in this person. The sport psychologist will usually gain the respect of the staff for working in this way.

Ultimately, they can only be effective in their work if they are able to communicate appropriately with all players and staff. Whilst the form, level and amount of communication can be controlled and even pre-scribed by the manager and senior staff, the sport psychologist would not be operating authentically, and would be failing to live up to their most important personal values, if they failed to engage in any type of dialogue with a person facing a critical moment. This is not merely about satisfying the duties listed on a job description, or meeting pro-fessional codes of conduct. Ultimately, the decision to work in certain ways with a player in this type of situation is based on what values the sport psychologist adheres to, and their philosophy of practice.

VALUES AND IDENTITY

Because of the particular demands placed upon the sport psychologist operating in high-level professional football there is a need for practi-tioners to have strong applied skills and possess excellent theoretical knowledge. One of the critiques of the education and training of many in sport psychology is that they are either highly competent in carrying out research or that they are particularly strong in terms of applied deliv-ery. According to Nesti (2004), much of this is related to the content of educational curricula and the accreditation systems currently in place.

Within counselling psychology and psychotherapy, the notion of the scientist-practitioner has long been recognized as an ideal for those doing applied work. According to Pilgrim and Treacher (1992), the scientist-practitioner is skilled and competent in the delivery of therapeutic interventions and has a thorough knowledge of psychological theory upon which these are based. This ensures that psychologists have the substance of theory to guide their work, whilst being highly skilled in delivery to a range of clients and groups. Within sport psychology there are many examples of outstanding practitioners who lack depth of knowledge in relation to underpinning psychological theory. Such individuals, whilst often being highly effective because of their personal qualities and extensive experience of performance sport, are often limited because they cannot locate their work within broader psychological frameworks or theoretical perspectives.

The identity of sport psychologists in Premiership football is vital to how their work will be received and perceived by staff and players. If the sport psychologist is working full time within the club there will be a different set of opportunities and challenges to face. It may be harder for the sport psychologist to convince players that his work with them will be completely confidential. On the other hand, it may be easier to build trust and to develop closer working relationships with both players and staff who can assist their work. The identity that I have usually been able to adopt has been one that is congruent with my understanding of the role of a sport psychologist in Premiership football. By operating part time but from within the club, usually on three to four days a week, I have been able to operate as an outsider who is on the inside. This allows the psychologist to enter into the day-to-day world of players and staff whilst maintaining a necessary distance to be able to gain the trust of players on issues like confidentiality and integrity.

The identity of the sport psychologist in this type of environment is not something that can be lived only when on duty. In many ways, this is quite similar to professions such as medicine, teaching and the church where there is a need to embody and be personally convincing in a vocation. It is no exaggeration to claim that beyond technical skill, theoretical knowledge and personal qualities, the professional whose work is a vocation is always on duty. In one sense, it is possible to say that for these individuals and sport psychologists, 'who we are is what we do'. In other words, our values and professional ethics must be part

160

of who we are, integral to how we see ourselves, and in that sense part of the deepest core of ourselves. It is this type of demanding identity that will ensure that the scepticism and negative perceptions of psychology and sport psychology so often experienced can be ameliorated by the credibility of the *person* of the sport psychologist.

According to both Maslow (1968) and the existential psychology approach from which humanistic psychology is partly derived, identity relates to the meaning that we attribute to our existence. The existential psychology view is divided into those who emphasize that since we can freely choose any values we wish, we can therefore determine who we are – our identity is totally in our own hands. The most famous (or infamous, depending on your point of view) individual associated with this perspective is the French writer and philosopher Jean-Paul Sartre. The other dominant approach within the existential position is also equally interested in the importance of meaning, values and identity. However, advocates of this position (Marcel 1948; Van Kaam 1969) in general psychology, and within sport psychology (Nesti 2004), argue that there are human values that are universally true, although how these are expressed and *encountered* might differ according to culture, place and history, and that the authentic human being is one whose identity is congruent with these values.

These psychologists claim that the identity of human beings is not something over which we have total freedom, and that our task is to live consistently with these values as we develop our identity. The sport psychologist who accepts this conception of identity will face anxiety frequently because of the challenges associated with meeting the demands of these values in daily life. For example, if honesty is something universally to be sought, desirable and true, then where a sport psychologist does not embody this value in his dealings with players and staff, the result will be existential anxiety and possibly a feeling of guilt. This anxiety, however, can be constructive, even if it feels uncomfortable.

Where people do not avoid the need to make choices to more fully and authentically meet the value of honesty in their psychological work they will be able to move past this anxiety and deepen their commitment to this value in their dealings with people, no matter how difficult this is to carry out. The harsh and at times brittle environment of top-level professional sport and Premiership football in particular, will mean that existential anxiety is encountered on a daily basis by the sport psychologist who attempts to live these universal values as consistently as possible. For some, anxiety about this level of authenticity will cause them to withdraw, compromise, or find ways to get around the problem. According to May (1977) – the first psychologist to write about the existential perspective on anxiety – any decision to avoid the anxiety associated with staying true to one's values will ultimately lead to a weaker sense of self and a fractured identity. Where a person or the sport psychologist chooses to act in this way continuously, they may even develop what May (1977) has referred to as neurotic anxiety.

If this seems to be a rather dramatic account of the importance of identity in relation to the values and working practices of a sport psychologist in Premiership football, it is worth remembering that research on identity in relation to athletes has concluded that problems can arise where there is a failure to develop our identity in line with sound values throughout our lives. Although the research of Brewer *et al.* (1993) does not precede from an existential psychology perspective, it does highlight the problems that arise where athletes avoid a proper exploration of identity as they progress in their sport lives. The work of Brewer *et al.* describes the problems that can arise from having a strong athletic identity, that is, one where sport performers see themselves solely in terms of sport and no longer consider that they have an identity beyond this. Apart from the restrictions that this places on an individual to consider other important sources of meaning in their lives beyond sport and sport-related experiences, this type of strong athletic identity can bring considerable problems when young sport performers fail to make the grade (Brown and Potrac 2009) or upon retirement from the sport or within career transitions (Pummell *et al.* 2008).

Accordingly, many staff and players in professional football are looking for an authentic individual who happens to have the skills, competencies and knowledge of sport psychology. In this sense, the wish is not for a sport psychologist per se but for a person of integrity who knows themselves (i.e. has a high degree of self-knowledge) and who clearly has knowledge and skills around psychological factors relating to performance sport *that they as players and staff do not possess.* This final point is extremely important. The identity of the sport psychologist working in this demanding level of sport must be about both aspects of what it is to be a professional. The psychologist should have a personal identity and set of values of a professional individual pursuing a vocation, and must also be highly knowledgeable about the discipline of psychology and be able, when called upon, to provide staff and players with a richer, more in-depth and ultimately more veracious answer to a particular situation, event or problem.

8

FOOTBALL LESSONS

IMPLICATIONS FOR OTHER PROFESSIONAL TEAM SPORTS

Working as a sport psychologist in any elite level professional sport environment places special demands upon the sport psychologist. Some of these relate to the rapidity of decision making, the impact of high levels of money, and the high level of competitiveness within the Premiership. This competitive spirit exists between teams, managers and players at the same club, and even on occasion between staff within individual clubs.

It goes without saying that to survive and thrive in this type of culture sport psychologists must possess a high level of confidence in their skills and knowledge. This will not be enough, however. Of equal if not greater importance, they must be mentally tough (Crust 2007), resilient, courageous (Corlett 1996b) and be prepared to live through many critical moments (Nesti and Littlewood [in press]). In addition, they will struggle to deliver an effective service unless they are willing to confront the existential anxiety (Nesti 2004) that will be faced frequently when they propose new ideas or attempt to change beliefs and practices. Without having a strong sense of self it will be extremely hard to act in an authentic way. Although necessary to the work of a psychologist, being authentic can sometimes come at great personal and professional cost in these often abrasive high-performance cultures.

The concept of authenticity and its relationship to anxiety and identity are vital to being able to deliver a useful and ethical service in professional sport. The guide below is provided by way of a summary of the key skills, qualities and attributes that must be developed by the sport psychologist to operate effectively in this work. However, the acquisition of these skills and qualities will often involve specific moments of existential anxiety. This will be experienced by the sport psychologist who hopes to offer something that differs from what other staff may contribute. Time and again, they must suggest possible solutions to the problems they are attempting to address. This often means that they will be offering something new, or at least pointing out that change must be made to improve matters. This extends to work with individual players, staff, smaller groups and the team as a whole.

The solutions proposed by the sport psychologist in these situations could be more precisely described as 'creative' in that they aim to bring form to something that looks like chaos, or give shape and meaning to assist the achievement of genuine progress. Creative behaviour always involves accepting the discomfort of anxiety about the unknown whilst being sufficiently courageous to follow the task through. This means taking personal responsibility for actions and ideas, which according to May (1975), always involves courage. The authentic person describes someone who is prepared to say and do things they believe in rather than someone whose aim is to survive and keep their heads down, or follow the party line. Such a sport psychologist will be courageous enough to offer guidance, ideas and advice to those who welcome it, and, equally importantly, to those less receptive.

This chapter looks at some of the important issues that a sport psychologist may have to deal with working in elite professional team sport environments. Although sports like Rugby Union, Rugby League and cricket at professional levels will provide some unique challenges for the sport psychologist delivering a service, many of the demands faced will be similar to those confronting the psychologist in Premiership football or elite professional football generally. Many of the topics covered below apply equally to the work of the sport psychologist who is working in a performance enhancement role in professional sport, whether in the UK, Europe, North America or elsewhere. Although there are several different perceptions around what constitutes sport psychology, and the value of having sport psychologists across different professional sports, there is little doubt that professional sport shares

166

many common values and elements of practice rarely seen in lower-level or amateur sports.

Because of this, it is argued that many of the points discussed here are for the most part relevant to a broad range of professional team sport environments, irrespective of specific factors such as, culture, gender, nationality, social class and history, and tradition.

MAKING FRIENDS: THE PLAYERS

Working with first team players

a. Previous experience of working with sport psychologists will influence players' views of their worth and the usefulness of their work. Many will have previously come across 'guru'-type figures often lacking formal qualifications in sport psychology and psychology, and who may be guilty of offering a simplistic and superficial service. Sometimes a player will have benefited from the input they received from these types of individuals, and may be disappointed or even frustrated to find that a particular psychologist does not offer the same type of support.

b. Players are not a homogeneous group, no matter how cohesive the team is, or how much they have achieved together. There is usually a hierarchy based on experience, level of clubs played at previously, perceived ability, level of wages, nature of contract and influence with the manager. Where players from the top of the hierarchy 'buy in' to the sport psychologist and their work, it can have a galvanizing impact on the other players. They may be more prepared to listen and engage with what the sport psychologist has to offer because of the example shown by senior players and those they admire personally or respect professionally.

c. Trust can be lost with players very quickly. In general, elite-level professional sport performers often develop a protective barrier around themselves because they have seen, or believe, that there are many people who are prepared to use them for their own ends, no matter the difficulties this produces for the player. Trust must be built up over the long term. Consistent behaviour, integrity and confidentiality will be the bedrock for this. The sport psychologist must also be perceived as someone who makes a difference.

d. High-level players and sport performers know through experience that their sport performances and broader lives are inextricably linked. They view themselves holistically, even though many sport psychologists, especially in academic institutions, seem prepared to engage only in reductionist positivist research. Sport psychologists must expect to discuss anything and everything from a player's life that the player thinks has an important affect on their performance as a professional athlete. This is not about working directly to help a player suffering with clinical issues, if a player suffers from these, since few sport psychologists are qualified to deal with such matters. However, it does mean that everything else is on the agenda, provided that it is always clear that the focus is ultimately related to improving performance.

Clubs will not employ sport psychologists who only deal with teaching players psychological techniques, or, conversely, who make it clear that they are not in the business of helping to make better performance more likely. If a player thinks the sport psychologist is not interested in performance, he will believe he has been wasting his time. Sport psychologists are not in a position to offer a caring-only role (Andersen 2009), or a narrow performance-only focus in elite professional sport. If they do, they will eventually be viewed as irrelevant, or possibly no different from a coach. Either way, their days will be numbered.

Players have egos. This is necessary to withstand such frequently encountered experiences as being dropped from the team, sold to other clubs or being pilloried in the media for a missed tackle or fluffed shot on goal. However, a strong ego can also get in the way of being able to do good sport psychology work with the player. This is where it will be vital that the sport psychologist truly understands that empathy means to stand in the other's place and see the world through their eyes. Ego defence mechanisms abound in high-level professional sport. With so much at stake and the desire to avoid being identified as the culprit when failure occurs, rationalizations, repression, reaction formation and sublimation (Freud 1991) are commonplace.

Although Freud did not work in professional sport, these constructs from his psychoanalytical approach are pervasive in this environment.

e. In some sports like professional football where there is a great deal of machismo (Richardson *et al.* 2004), sport psychologists should not expect much in the way of positive feedback from the players they work with. Many in professional teams sports will view psychology in a somewhat ambivalent way. There will always be an undercurrent of feeling that, really, it is mostly for the weak, those in trouble, or the desperate.

Interestingly, individuals who are deeply confident, authentic, well grounded and highly talented are likely to be the only group of players who consistently provide constructive and positive feedback to the sport psychologist. This paradox appears to be somewhat of a chicken and egg scenario. In other words, are some players able to acknowledge the importance of sport psychologists because they are confident as high achievers, or are they confident high achievers because they are open to learning what they can from all of the situations and individuals they have encountered, including sport psychologists?

f. Players often understand that sport psychology input will take a fair amount of time to impact on behaviours and thinking. They know this, since they have experienced it personally in all other areas of performance on their way to the top. Some managers, coaches and others may not see it this way, however, and will expect significant and rapid change.

g. Some players will be afraid of working with a sport psychologist one to one because they will have to face up to their failings and share these with another person. Although clarification and dialogue can bring about good feelings (and positive change eventually), it can also be very uncomfortable initially, especially where discussion is about something important to the player (as if a professional player would give up their valuable time to talk about something that is peripheral in their lives!). The sport psychologist must expect that they will also be viewed as an instrument of fear by some. Much better this, though, than to be ignored or considered an unreal individual who thinks that healing, growth, change or learning can never take place without some degree of fear, anxiety, stress and doubt (Nesti 2007).

A player with some of these emotions and cognitions is someone who at least knows what is at stake. Self-awareness and self-knowledge beyond this are not easily attained, but the desire to develop the self cannot be evaded for long without this also causing pain and hurt. As Kierkegaard (1944 [1844]) pointed out, avoiding the challenge to grow and learn by diminishing the self does not eliminate fear and trembling (angst); in fact, it makes these feelings even more powerful and crippling.

The sport psychologist must be fully prepared to expect that many elite sport performers, in spite of their highly confident and positive public personae, are afraid that 'some day I will be found out and it will all come crashing down'. This type of fear is common and has a constructive aspect to it where it keeps the sport performer hungry to improve. It can also provide a basis for the vital quality of humility.

MAKING FRIENDS: THE STAFF

Developing professional relationships with the staff

a. The sport psychologist will usually have been appointed by the manager with the support of the chairman or chief executive. The relationship between the manager and the sport psychologist is absolutely crucial to the latter's experience at the club and the possibility of achieving their aims. The support of their manager can ensure that the sport psychologist will be accepted quickly by players and staff and will help his work to be taken seriously and viewed positively. Conversely, a difficult or fractured relationship between manager and their sport psychologist will make it virtually impossible to carry out effective work. If these two individuals have very different views about the long-term goals of the club or team, or do not agree with the shorter-term requirements to help the team achieve success, the sport psychologist will not last long in the job.

b. Although the manager is key, the sport psychologist will be able to do much more work if the assistant manager, first team coach and other senior coaching staff value his input and welcome him into the team on a professional and personal level. If important individuals in this group do not think highly of the sport psychologist or the activities he pursues, depending on their relationship with the manager, the sport psychologist may eventually be removed from the post. It is important to remember that many coaches view themselves as competent applied psychologists, based on their experience as players and coaches. Failure to acknowledge this and work with it, instead of against it, is to increase the odds against the sport psychologist being able to carry out his function properly.

c. It is very important that the sport psychologist can develop close professional relationships with the sport science and sport medicine staff. This group of individuals, at least in terms of formal qualifications, is often the closest to the sport psychologist. They can be extremely valuable in helping sport psychologists achieve their tasks. If they do not respect the person of the sport psychologist or his professional role, this can be even more destructive than difficulties with the coaching staff. This is because it is expected that similarly qualified individuals with specialist sport and exercise science knowledge will be able to work well together because of a shared philosophy and educational experiences.

   Where this does not happen, managers and other senior staff may conclude that it is to the result of poor skills and personal qualities in the sport psychologist, or because the psychologist is not adequately qualified to work at this level of excellence. This may be an unfair or inaccurate assessment, and can more easily occur where the psychologist is a new member of staff, part-time employee or operates as an external consultant.

d. It is essential to remember that individuals from within the staff will discuss many topics with the sport psychologist and expect complete confidentiality. This means that they may be told very important things relating to personal and professional matters by their colleagues because they are a psychologist, rather than a sport psychologist per se. This can happen at any time or situation, but increases in likelihood the more the sport psychologist socializes with the staff. Sport psychologists are always on duty but must be seen as one of the group at the same time. They must get involved in the social life of their staff colleagues at some level at least, and be seen as ordinary persons with a passion for sport and other topics.

However, they should not be surprised if their colleagues tell them in confidence about sensitive and important matters when they are out socializing together. These could be about work-related matters related to players or other staff, or could be about personal situations and relationships. Such experiences will have to be handled by the sport psychologist in a sensitive, professional and constructive way – not an easy thing to do in a lively pub or late-night bar. This can place great demands on sport psychologists, and can be a significant challenge, especially when they wish to be off duty as well!

YOUTHFUL ENERGY

Working with young players and staff

a. This group of players represent the future of the club. In some sports like professional football, especially in the Premiership, young players are finding it increasingly difficult to advance to the first team. To counteract this, investing in developing young talent has become ever more systematic and planned. The sport psychologist must remember that young players are not a single group but that they contain a huge range of individuals with different levels of emotional, physical and psychological maturity. This means that alongside the individualized approach taken with first team players, special allowances will have to be made to accommodate the differences that exist, for example, between nine-year-old novice players and more mature and experienced sixteen-year-olds.

b. A sport psychologist may find that staff in an academy or youth section is more positive than first team staff about the value of

172

psychology in helping their young athletes to improve. This greater acceptance is related to the developmental focus of those involved in youth sport, and to the fact that the coaches in elite sports environments often highlight psychological factors as the most important variables in predicting the success of young players (Gould *et al.* 2002). Sport psychologists will also find that they are afforded more time to carry out their tasks and see the benefits of their work in this environment.

c. Although the staff support may be strong and the environment conducive to sport psychology, work with the young sport performers themselves in groups, or individually, is no easy task. Typically, they would much rather play, train or perform physical tasks than do more educationally focused work including sport psychology. Where this work can be delivered alongside the coach in practical sessions, or integrated into training, many objections to sport psychology melt away. Delivering to groups or one to one requires great skill from the sport psychologist given the following constraints are often in place:

   ■ antipathy to anything that is classroom-based or looks like school
   ■ a wide range of intelligence, emotional maturity, motivation, interest and attention span, in even apparently homogeneous groups
   ■ limitations due to language skills, lack of vocabulary, desire to conform, family problems, school demands
   ■ fear that sport psychologists are not there to help them develop but to aid team selection or influence who progresses to first team and professional ranks.

d. With young sport performers or players, a sport psychologist will be more likely to be perceived positively if the manager, head coaches, first team players and youth coaches see this work as important and useful. Such a perception can be developed by the manager or senior players speaking to youth performers to explain exactly why the mental side of the sport is so important and encouraging them to fully engage in the service offered by the sport psychologist. Support from key staff or respected players is all the more important when the sport psychologist has not formerly been a high-level performer in the sport.

e. Today's youth player may become tomorrow's great new find! Having been a small part of someone's progress to high-level achievement feels good, brings confidence and helps spread the message that psychological input is important and helpful.

THE PUBLIC

Media, fans and agents

a. It is important to remember that many in the media are intrigued about the role of sport psychologists in elite professional sport. Often their views range from a deep level of scepticism about how psychologists can affect sport performance to a belief that all top performers should have their own personal sport psychologist. The media portrayal of sport psychology will often reflect those two very different perspectives, sometimes in the same news item or article. Sport psychologists must take care in their dealings with the media. The best approach is to adopt a low-key stance, resist making grand claims about the importance of the discipline, and insist that their work is not about clinical issues or mystical techniques, but like coaches, aimed at short-term help and longer-term development of players to assist individual and team performance. All other talk is potentially dangerous, and can undo much that may have been achieved in getting players and staff to accept and welcome the legitimacy of having a sport psychologist on board. Psychologists and sport psychology are deeply interesting topics to many people, but there remain many misunderstandings about what the discipline is about and what the role entails.

Attempting to explain this in a short interview or brief article is best avoided in most cases. However, more lengthy interviews with the media, or in-depth articles from sympathetic and well-informed journalists, can be a great help.

b. Many supporter groups will have people with a wealth of knowledge about the sport, team and club. In addition, a usual cross-section of supporters will include individuals who have played or performed the sport at an excellent level, and people with a diverse range of skills and knowledge. Sport psychologists may find that they learn as much from dialogue with fans as the fans do from them. If the opportunity arises, sport psychologists should meet with supporters groups to learn about their views on the team, individual players and staff, and to gain an appreciation of how aware they are about psychological factors important for success.

c. Sport psychologists must ensure, in dealing with media or support-ers groups, that they stay on message at all times – that is, the club or team's message rather than their own!

d. Agents are common in most elite professional sports environments. Some are highly qualified professionals who operate ethically and with integrity. Others may not always act in this way. A good and professional agent can be an excellent ally for the sport psycho-logist where they lend their support to work carried out with the player. A sport psychologist may find that even when an agent is not particularly keen for their player to work with a psychologist, good work can still be done. All agents, after all, want their charges to do well, and if the club finds it important that players work with psychologists, then, despite their possible reservations, agents will usually be prepared go along with this.

X FACTOR SPECIALISTS

Club chaplains and liaison officers

a. Club chaplains can be a valuable source of pastoral support for players and staff, whether these are religiously minded or not. Sport psychologists share a pastoral identity with chaplains, again, irre-spective of their own attitudes towards religion and belief. Players in particular will tend to see similarities between chaplains and sport psychologists; one deals with the soul, one with the mind, but both are interested in developing persons and even team spirit and character.

b. Sport psychologists should not allow their own faith, lack of it, or attitude towards religious belief stop them from working collaboratively wherever they can with someone whose vocation, in many ways like good sport psychologists, sets them apart from other staff usually found in elite professional sports organizations. Often the chaplain has been at the club or team for many years, and will have a wealth of knowledge. They will often have been able to develop excellent links with key people in the organization. Sometimes the chaplain has been brought in to the club by the manager or head coach; most usually it is because the owner, members of the Board, or senior management on the business side of the club have appointed them. The sport psychologist will do well to remember this if they feel unable to work with them, even in a small way, because of their own prejudice about people with a religious belief.

c. Liaison officers may be able to help the sport psychologist through their knowledge of the lifestyle and domestic circumstances of players. Some sports organizations task liaison duties to external specialist companies, whilst others appoint staff to full-time roles within the club. The sport psychologist should cultivate a close working relationship with these individuals who are not infrequently the first to be aware of potential problems facing players which, if not addressed, could impact on them psychologically and undermine their performances.

BEING A BOFFIN

Carrying out research

a. Research opportunities abound when working as a sport psychologist in elite professional sport. There is a dearth of published papers on professional sport because of the difficulty of getting access to this population, issues of confidentiality and a desire to keep secrets 'in house' and beyond the prying eyes of the media or other competitors in the sport. If the sport psychologist does engage in research, great care must be taken to ensure this is primarily to assist the club or team.

It goes without saying that the key individuals must be fully informed about the research, permission sought for publication of results and intellectual property rights respected. Many elite professional sport organizations are suspicious of the purposes behind much of the research proposed to them. They appear to believe that, in the final analysis, although researchers have achieved their aims, the club or team has gained little or nothing from what has been a time-consuming exercise. Sport psychologists should always make sure that any potential research project is carefully explained to ensure that the benefits to the club are fully articulated. It is also important that this work is not carried out at the expense of other more immediate and essential activities.

For sport psychologists based at universities this issue is one of the most difficult they may face. If they get it wrong and they may find their contract with the sport organization will be terminated, and depending on the research and where results have been published, they may face the threat of legal action and have their professional reputation severely damaged.

b. Existing published research must be made accessible by the sport psychologist for the benefit of the club. This may involve summarizing studies carried out in other sport organizations and attempting to ensure that a full and accurate understanding is achieved. This can be used to inform changes in practice or to lend support to existing initiatives. The rapid growth in the use of sports science and performance analysis within elite level professional sport means that coaches and others are more ready to seek evidence upon which to base their decisions. Yet within sports such as professional football there remains a healthy degree of scepticism around the value of research data and so-called evidence-based practice. This is because staff are aware that research carries its own limitations. These limitations are due to the fact that data and results must always be subject to interpretation, and that a choice must be made about data analysis or data collection techniques, which inevitably impacts on what is discovered.

In addition, this positive scepticism is a reflection of understanding the differences between natural science and human science paradigms (Giorgi 2000). Put simply, there is often a good understanding that strict cause-and-effect relationships do not exist in human activities, and especially in areas such as sport where individual motivations, passions and intentions are impossible to fully control or predict. This view is taken by most in elite-level sport in relation to all available performance data. In terms of psychological research, there is an even greater willingness to interpret this more loosely. It is understood that it can be useful in pointing towards possible solutions or influencing factors. However, there is no expectation that such research will be able to provide the final word on any matter.

Paradoxically, in many ways, this critical perspective of psychology and psychological data adopted in professional sport is more authentically academic than the perspective taken by some researchers within university settings. Sport psychologists who fail to take a genuinely academic and critical perspective when called upon to translate the research of others, or when explaining their own research findings, will lose much credibility in the world of professional sport.

The more advanced the level of performance, the greater the understanding of the benefits and weaknesses of the scientific method (Kuhn 1977). Coaches in particular in such organizations often possess a high degree of craft knowledge and base their practice on evidence. This in turn is derived from formal knowledge gained through years of practice and reflection. This type of thinking will be carried out alone, or sometimes in dialogue with other coaches. In many ways the environment of high-level professional team sport provides the impetus to ensure that staff are constantly thinking about how they can improve performance and reflecting on what they have discovered through close analysis of performance data relating to matches and training.

To suggest that reflective practice (Knowles *et al.* 2007) is a new skill for this group is to fail to appreciate that without devoting considerable effort to thinking carefully about why certain things have occurred, and how these can be made better is to put one's job in jeopardy. In common with other highly pressurized professional jobs such as medicine, law and teaching, it can be argued that reflective practice takes place constantly, and that practice is always informed by evidence. This may take the form of empirical research, emerge from literature about relevant professional practice, or be based on longitudinal studies (otherwise known as the traditions of the profession). The sport psychologist will find that despite a concern that research is oriented towards improving performance, the higher the level of sports organization, the greater will be the awareness that such research may only be able to offer a limited number of tentative suggestions.

Sport psychologists must work closely with clubs, coaches and others to ensure that all research they carry out is clearly aimed at assisting the club to improve performance. Attempting to do anything else will be viewed negatively. Despite this, the subtle and advanced level of understanding about how performance can be improved in top professional sports organizations will mean that a broad range of topics can be studied. There also tends to be a clear recognition that when it comes to top-level performance, the whole life of an athlete from a physical, psychological, emotional and social dimension will be important.

c. There may also be an opportunity either with small groups of staff or at an individual level to provide educational sessions focusing on the value of research and its strengths and limitations. For some staff who possibly have not acquired higher-level academic qualifications, this could prove a beneficial experience allowing them to develop greater knowledge and understanding of research in their sport. There are clear opportunities to bring researchers in from universities and elsewhere to present their research to the staff at the club or sports organization. The sport psychologist can use these occasions to help reinforce change in practice or to stimulate new ideas.

Researchers could have an opportunity to develop collaborative projects with the sport organization or club as a result of these meetings and presentations. This is another practical method that a sport psychologist can use to facilitate knowledge transfer between universities, other research centres and professional sport clubs.

The focus of the research could be on physiology, nutrition, sport psychology or other sport science-related disciplines.

d. The sport psychologist may be able to develop links between the club and university staff with expertise in business and strategic management. Although there are several excellent consultancies outside university settings that are able to help sports organizations develop their strategic thinking and performance environments, the cost of these services may be prohibitive. Universities are often able to provide a more competitive range of consultancy fees because they sometimes place great value on the research opportunities that can arise alongside the work they do for the sports organization.

    The sport psychologist may be able to build closer links with local universities and institutions of higher education to allow for staff secondments and student placements to take place. There is often an attractive public relations dimension to this as well. Universities are major employers and are increasingly populated by ever greater numbers of local students on full-time and part-time courses. Collaboration between local universities and elite professional sports clubs can be a source of pride for both organizations, and will usually be perceived favourably within the local area by the media, public and politicians. In this way, the sport psychologist can contribute to efforts that a club may be undertaking to strengthen their visibility in the local community, and to be seen as a positive factor in supporting the social and economic growth of a city or region.

e. It may also be possible for the sport psychologist to take a lead on the formation of collaborative research institutes between local universities and the elite professional sports organization. This could include other partners from health and local government sectors, and can extend to areas like sports medicine and community development. There will usually be several individuals in elite professional sports clubs who possess high levels of knowledge about local provision and expertise relating to their own discipline. For example, physiotherapy staff, nutritionists and fitness coaches will frequently have developed some level of contact with other individuals in different organizations locally who share their subject knowledge and professional qualifications.

180

However, the task of developing more formal links between individuals, and creating structures to facilitate more permanent collaborative initiatives may be something such individuals do not have the time or expertise to carry forward. Sport psychologists, on the other hand, may be the ideal candidates to address these types of projects (although not primarily about sport psychology) on behalf of the club since they often have some level of knowledge about sport science and sport medicine, and should possess good communication and organizational skills.

GETTING PAID

Remuneration, contracts, money, hours and conditions of work

a. Do not expect that there will be a clearly defined, formal job description at the club for the role of sport psychologist. This could be because the sports organization has never employed someone in this type of position before, or that this work has been delivered by an external consultant on an *ad hoc* basis. This situation presents a great opportunity for the incoming sport psychologist to write their own draft job description. This can then be used in meetings with chairman, manager and other key staff to agree a final job description.

b. Although many elite-level professional sports organizations are relatively wealthy, the sport psychologist should not anticipate that they will receive a high level of remuneration. At least until they have established themselves within the club and proved their worth, the salary of the sport psychologist in these environments may initially be significantly less than they would receive in a lecturing position or permanent contract at a regional or national governing body of sport. The big money in professional sport is concentrated on players' salaries, managers and senior coaching staff. Many others in sport science, physiotherapy and performance analysis posts, for example, may find themselves paid less than they would expect outside professional sport.

c. It is quite usual to work very long hours in this environment and to be expected to change plans at short notice to come into training or attend meetings. Within the pressured environment of a Premiership football club, the staff expect to be available at all times. This means that from the start of pre-season training in early July until the end of season in mid- to late May the following year, the club demands 100 per cent of staff's time. For a sport psychologist used to working in less intense environments or more managed and planned work situations, this can take some adjustment. Again, sport psychologists employed on a part-time basis by the club will usually find that they are still expected to operate with a 24/7 mentality.

THE BIG TEN

Key contextual variables that the sport psychologist must keep in mind when working in elite professional sports organizations

1. The sport psychologist should always attempt to provide a counter-cultural service. In other words, they should avoid 'going native' at all costs. There should be no misunderstanding about who they are, how they behave, or what they say and, ultimately, what they do – they should not be confused with any other member of staff. As psychologists, they must ask the questions that others are reluctant to ask, and, of equal importance, help influence and guide the answers so that they are in line with sound psychological principles and theory. It will be uncomfortable at times operating in this way, but not to do so will most likely result in one of two outcomes: being quickly ignored or being viewed eventually as a luxury, as someone who does not contribute to enhancing the performance of the team.

   More dramatically, to behave in this way is to guarantee losing the job. The psychologist must always remember that we live in a psychological age (Vitz 1994) and that this means, amongst other things, that there is an unrealistically high level of expectation of what benefits psychology can bring. Any goodwill and high level of interest will rapidly diminish if the sport psychologist spends time telling coaches, players and others about things that they already know. The sport psychologist must have something different to say, and be capable of finding the appropriate words to articulate this to a range of different audiences. They must endeavour to provide advice, insight and inspiration based on the very best psychological theory and research. This must be offered during the best of times as well as in the midst of the most difficult periods.

2. The sport psychologist must get ready to be insulted, misunder-stood, ignored, denigrated, seen as a 'mole', a threat, as 'unreal', not sufficiently performance focused, and peripheral and lightweight.

3. Equally, sport psychologists must be prepared to be invited on to the 'top table' where major decisions are made and highly sensitive information is discussed. They must be ready to be consulted con-fidentially about players and key staff that they are working with, to be involved in contributing to discussions about team performance and selection, and involved in the recruitment of new staff. They must expect to discuss matters with players on important personal issues, and listen to highly sensitive and confidential material that the media and other parties would die for.

    The sport psychologist must also expect to be asked to men-tor staff with considerable experience in the sport, and to act as a confidant for senior individuals in the sport organization who may have a high public profile, both nationally and internationally. They should be primed to accept that they will sometimes be viewed as rather unusual, unorthodox, enigmatic, mystical, somewhat detached, and not really fully part of it all, but somehow important.

    Most of all, they should be prepared for the reality that all three of these very different experiences and perceptions can be encoun-tered several times in a normal day. This will place great demands on personal values, self-belief, knowledge, identity and integrity.

4. It is crucially important for job satisfaction, job security and to help the credibility of sport psychology to grow and improve that the sport psychologist is capable of offering something of depth and substance which nevertheless must be related to the world of elite professional sport. This will help for a number of reasons. First, it ensures that the sport psychologist will be able to offer something

different to other staff in the sports organization and will counter the criticism often expressed in elite-level sport that sport psychologists are experts in providing short-term, quick-fix answers that do not stand the test of time.

Second, this depth will ensure that the sport psychologist is able to help other staff to appreciate that sport psychology, and more generally the discipline of psychology itself, cannot be reduced to 'pop psychology' and the books on personal self-improvement that sell so well in our so-called postmodern, materialistic, consumer culture (Fforde 2009). The sport psychologist who is unafraid to search for the best answer even where this does not result in a simplistic or easily digestible message will ensure that they are not mistaken for a psychological guru.

Particularly within Premiership football, it is common to receive offers of help across a season from individuals who claim to have psychological skills and competence, despite possessing few recognized qualifications and lacking in experience. Many of these 'gurus' are former coaches or ex-players who have been impressed by the power of psychology through exposure to a menu of techniques that they may have personally benefited from. Such individuals can make great claims about the efficacy of their approach, and sometimes provide documentary evidence to suggest that they have had considerable experience and success at the highest levels.

Upon closer inspection, many of the claims are gross exaggerations. In professional sport, there is an appetite for charismatic individuals who promise easy and quick solutions to deep-rooted problems and challenges. The existence of such individuals provides the qualified sport psychologist with an opportunity to demonstrate how their theoretically richer, more in-depth, ethical and professional approach is of greater benefit in the short, medium and long term.

Sport psychologists, despite carefully explaining their roles, professional competence and what their qualifications allow them to do, will continue to find that players, staff, media and others will, on occasion, still see them as clinical psychologists or psychiatrists. Over time, and by showing the types of skills and knowledge that they possess, this misunderstanding will become less common.

However, even where most in elite professional sport are now

184

better informed about the function of a sport psychologist, it will still be possible to be described as the 'shrink', or the 'psycho'. This is a reflection of the confusion that is evident in society in general, and, it has to be said, is also prevalent within the disciplines of psychology and sport psychology. An example of this is the confusion that exists in the work of some sport psychologists who give the impression that clinical and counselling psychology are synonymous (Moore 2003), or that counselling and clinical psychologists deal with exactly the same issues (Anderson and Clarke 2002).

5. Sport psychologists must be ready to face the end, which will almost always be abrupt and ugly. Professional sport at the highest level, including Premiership football, is subject to many of the negative forces that are currently impinging on social, economic, business, political and public life in Western societies. In other words, professional sport is subject to the same type of desocialization that is 'a particular condition that accompanies post modern societies where values are considered relative and consumerism and philosophical materialism are the dominant forces' (Fforde 2009).

Within this type of framework, individual rights and desires are sovereign. The notion of loyalty to community, and that people and groups are more important than financial and material success is largely alien in this kind of atmosphere. The values that tend to dominate in such environments will be those associated with short-term gains, and a focus on ends rather than means. There will often be a flexible approach to ethics and the dismissal of words such as loyalty, integrity and humility as being essentially a bit out of date and rather arcane. Elite-level sports organizations, including Premiership football clubs, are operating at the cutting edge of this new order. Although there are courageous individuals who attempt to act according to time-honoured values and try to resist the processes which seek to elevate personal self-aggrandisement over individual and community success, it is difficult to maintain these values within an increasingly fast-moving, pragmatic and largely utilitarian environment. The sport psychologist, like most other staff and sport performers in these cultures, will eventually lose their jobs, whether they have been successful or not.

The desire for quicker and greater achievement will guarantee that long-term job security becomes harder and harder to attain. From a practical point of view this means that sport psychologists must always devote effort and energy to prepare for their next job, since this will either be a decision forced upon them by others, or will be something they need to take forward in order to remain in work.

For those individuals used to operating in more stable environments where there is a greater recognition of the importance of building staff teams for the longer term, working in professional sport will be a significantly different experience. In addition, when psychologists move on to other opportunities, are sacked or their contract comes to an end, usually there will be little contact from their previous colleagues. Although individual situations may differ, this often happens because elite professional sport, and Premiership football in particular, is now moving at such a rapid pace and the pressures to succeed are so great, that individuals must focus quickly on their own situation to ensure their continual survival in work. This brutal environment has arguably contributed to the realization that this can help create a climate of fear, insecurity and a lack of trust. At an individual level this may mean that there is a tendency to look after one's own interests first, and try not to think about the misfortunes that have affected others since there is no spare capacity, psychologically or emotionally, to engage in such reflections. Such a utilitarian and functional approach to people is increasingly commonplace in modern Western societies where various forces are influencing people to consider the value of life primarily in terms of what it can contribute to society in terms of economic benefit. For many sport psychologists who are grounded in humanistic, existential and other philosophically informed perspectives, working in elite professional sport may be a wonderful environment in which to encourage people to learn and grow, but, not infrequently, it is also a harsh and bitter place to leave.

6. Sport psychologists have to decide what legacy they want to leave behind. It is easy to become lost in the relentless processes that can take over even where a sport psychologist is intensely focused on the essentials to be delivered. Particularly during difficult moments where there are major changes taking place, or continual uncertainty

186

surrounding staff or players across the organization as a whole, the psychologist must keep in mind that eventually he will not be in post.

This realization should provide the impetus to think carefully about what legacy they would like to leave. This might be a new approach to the delivery of sport psychology support with the players, the inclusion of psychological assessment within the recruitment of staff and players, or in having been able to increase the understanding of a number of key staff or players in relation to psychological factors.

This could even extend to the person of the psychologist themselves. For example, they may hope that when they depart from the club or team, that some individuals there will have a more positive view of sport psychologists even if they remain less convinced about the discipline of sport psychology. This could happen, for example, where some of the staff and players recognize that the sport psychologist has been able to understand the contextual demands of an elite professional sport environment, and where the psychologist's personal qualities are remembered positively, even though some of their work is viewed less favourably. To a certain extent, the sport psychologist will be unable to guarantee a particular legacy. The culture of the sports organization, understanding of the value of sport psychology, and the different views held by individuals, staff and players in the club will ultimately determine how much of this legacy can be detected.

However, for sport psychologists, the professional satisfaction will be in remembering that they had an overarching vision of what they were trying to do and that they worked towards this in the hope that when they are no longer involved, some of their work would remain behind.

Related to this, sport psychologists must be careful not to lose sight of the longer term and broader aims that motivate them in their work. It is important not to lose yourself in the 'fluff' of the celebrity world or the glamour and profile that inevitably accompanies the world of elite professional sport, especially in high-profile sports like Premiership football. However, this does not mean that you should not join the 'party' and take a full part in celebrations when the mood takes you. There are many people who would wish to work in professional sport because of the culture of celebrity attached to it and the prestige that can be accrued. In reality, many of the staff and players who work in these types of environments are often little interested in this aspect. Sport psychologists would do well to keep this in mind and ensure that no one can accuse them of being in it for the enhancement of their public profile. Professional players at the highest level of the game often refer to those with these types of motives as being individuals who are,'living the dream'. It is important that the sport psychologist is never accused of being such a person, although it is both professionally legitimate and appealing to colleagues if they show from time to time how aware they are that they are fortunate to be working in such an exciting and rewarding situation.

7. To maintain focus, motivation and desire for work in such a demanding place as a Premiership football club or within elite professional sport in general, it is vital that sport psychologists devote a significant amount of time to preparing for their next job, project or role. This could mean that they might construct their own bespoke continuing professional development programme to help them to develop new knowledge and additional skills to make them attractive to future employers.

This can be facilitated by study visits and mini exchanges. As a sport psychologist working in elite professional sport or Premiership football, there will be no lack of offers from other teams, clubs or sports organizations to meet, share information and develop new ideas. This can often be carried out with the support of the manager, senior staff or the club the sport psychologist is currently working at.

The club may be willing to support such training and development because they recognize that benefits will accrue to both the individual psychologist and possibly to the work that they perform for the team. It is useful to maintain links with other sport psychologists working in different sports. This will allow for a sharing of information and may bring new ideas that help keep a fresh approach to the work. It will ensure that the individual is less likely to be 'consumed with process', which can lead to demotivation and becoming stale.

8. Sport psychologists must be authentic – know who they are, what they stand for and their core values. They must strive to live according to this identity despite the constraints imposed on them in professional sports environments. This will allow them to successfully confront the existential anxiety which will be experienced daily as they carry out their role. The sport psychologist who lacks a strong sense of self, based on a high degree of self-knowledge, will find it very difficult to carry out work of a psychological nature with players and staff. There will also be the challenges associated with many of the cultural and operational factors that have been discussed in this book. The lack of understanding of their role, volatility of the environment, and other personal and professional challenges facing sport psychologists delivering within elite professional sport will test their values. In order to operate in an environment such as this, the sport psychologist will need a strong sense of self, which Nesti (2007) has argued should encompass sound and mature values that will allow the person to operate in a flexible way without compromising deeply held beliefs.

9. To be authentic will require courage. Courage is a personal quality that can be developed through facing up to the experience of challenging situations. The courageous act will require the sport psychologist to pursue a particular task, often without much support from others. Ultimately, sport psychologists will have to make these decisions alone. This will involve a careful scrutiny of what they hope to achieve, and why they are prepared to attempt this, whether it be welcomed by others, or perceived as unwelcome. In many ways being authentic is deeply rewarding, personally and professionally satisfying, and yet can be a very risky choice in these environments.

   Many staff, players and elite sport performers manage to survive in the medium term at least, through operating beneath the 'radar', or sometimes by adopting what appears to be a crude or cynical approach. This might mean that they remain silent in situations when they should speak out to offer a different view, or that they engage in tasks or behaviours they strongly disagree with in private. Unfortunately, use of such strategies is usually bought at great expense to the psychological health and well-being of the individual concerned. This may be one of the reasons why elite professional sports cultures contain sport performers, coaches, and others who seek to avoid the anxiety associated with being authentic through use of various addictive types of behaviour.

According to the existential psychology view (Nesti 2007), the sport psychologist who tries to be an authentic individual and constantly reveals their true self without fear of the repercussions will almost inevitably journey from 'hero to zero'. Orlick (2000) has used this phrase to describe the experiences of athletes facing retirement from sport, career-threatening injury, being cut from the team or sold by the club. The term can also describe the experience facing the sport psychologist who attempts to act authentically.

The dedication to following an honest and courageous stance in their work will sometimes result in their being viewed favourably and even as heroic examples to others. These same authentic behaviours at other times, however, may be much more problematic and can contribute to the sport psychologist being seen as someone to be ignored or even vilified.

10. A final note of caution for sport psychologists seeking to operate within elite professional sport is they must do all that they can to secure their contracts and remuneration packages as early as possible. This is because, despite the increasing commercialization of top-level professional sport, there are many examples of clubs suffering from financial instability and poor management of monetary resources.

There are a number of reasons contributing to this state of affairs, and there are many individuals within sports governing bodies, the government, the leagues and sports clubs themselves who are concerned by such situations and practices. Sport psychologists must take great care to secure their positions and salaries given what has happened in many areas of business, and within vast parts of public and political life over recent years. As Glendon (2006) has warned, ever increasing sums of money aligned to a dominant postmodern culture of relativism and a sceptical view about the possibility of truth itself, has contributed to reduced ethical standards and financial probity.

190

REFERENCES

Andersen, M. B. (ed.) (2000) *Doing Sport Psychology*, Champaign, IL: Human Kinetics.

—— (2005) 'Yeah, I work with Beckham': issues of confidentiality privacy and privilege in sport psychology service delivery', *Sport and Exercise Psychology Review*, 1: 5–13.

—— (2009) 'Performance enhancement as a bad start and a dead end: a parenthetical comment on Mellalieu and Lane', *The Sport and Exercise Scientist*, 20: 12–14.

Andersen, M. B. and Tod, D. (2006) 'When to refer athletes for counselling or psychotherapy', in J. Williams (ed.), *Applied Sport Psychology: personal growth to peak performance*, Palo Alto, CA: Mayfield Publishing Company, pp. 483–95.

Anderson, A. and Clarke, P. (2002) 'Afterword', in D. Lavallee and I. Cockerill (eds), *Counselling in Sport and Exercise Contexts*, Leicester: British Psychological Society, pp. 69–73.

Anderson, A., Miles, A., Robinson, P. and Mahoney, C. (2004). 'Evaluating the athlete's perception of the sport psychologist's effectiveness: what should we be assessing? *Psychology of Sport and Exercise*, 5: 255–77.

Aquinas, T. (1964) *Summa Theologiae*, New York: McGraw-Hill.

Balague, G. (1999) 'Understanding identity, value and meaning when working with elite athletes', *The Sport Psychologist*, 13: 89–98.

Barker, J. R. (1999) *The Discipline of Teamwork: participation and concretive control*. Newbury Park, CA: Sage.

Brady, C., Bolchover, D. and Sturgess, B. (2008) 'Managing in the talent economy: the football model for business', *California Management Review*, 50: 54–73.

Brewer, B. W., Van Raalte, J. L. and Linder, D. E. (1993) 'Athletic identity: Hercules' muscles or Achilles heel', *International Journal of Sport Psychology*, 24: 237–54.

Brown, G. and Potrac, P. (2009) 'You've not made the grade, son': deselection and identity disruption in elite level youth football', *Soccer and Society*, 10: 143–59.

Buber, M. (1958) *I and Thou,* trans. R. G. Smith, Edinburgh: T & T Clark, New York: Charles Scribner's Sons.

Bull, S. J., Albinson, J. G. and Sambrook, C. J. (1996) *The Mental Game Plan: getting psyched for sport*, Eastbourne: Sports Dynamics.

Carron, A. V. and Hausenblas, H. A. (1998) *Group Dynamics in Sport,* Morgantown, WV: Fitness Information Technology.

Caruso, I. A. (1964) *Existential Psychology: from analysis to synthesis*, London: Darton, Longman and Todd.

Chelladurai, P. and Trail, G. (2006) 'Styles of decision making in coaching', in J. Williams (ed.), *Applied Sport Psychology: personal growth to peak performance*, Palo Alto, CA: Mayfield Publishing Company, pp. 107–19.

Chesterton, G. K. (1993) *The Everlasting Man*, San Francisco, CA: Ignatius Press.

Clough, P. J., Earle, K. and Sewell, D. (2002) Mental toughness: the concept and its measurement, in I. Cockerill (ed.), *Solutions in Sport Psychology*, London: Thomson Publishing, pp. 32–43.

Cockerill, I. (ed.) (2002) *Solutions in Sport Psychology*, London: Thomson Publishing.

Corlett, J. (1996a) 'Sophistry, Socrates and sport psychology', *The Sport Psychologist*, 10: 84–94.

—— (1996b) 'Virtue lost: courage in sport', *Journal of the Philosophy of Sport*, 23: 45–57.

Crust, L. (2007) 'Mental toughness in sport: a review', *International Journal of Sport and Exercise Psychology*, 5: 270–90.

Csikszentmihalyi, M. (1975) *Beyond Boredom and Anxiety*, San Francisco, CA: Jossey-Bass.

—— (1992) *Flow: the psychology of happiness*, London: Rider Publications.

—— (1996) *Flow and the Psychology of Discovery and Invention*, New York: Harper Perennial.

Dale, G. (1996) 'Existential-phenomenology: emphasising the experience of the athlete in sport psychology research', *The Sport Psychologist*, 10: 158–71.

Deci, E. L. and Ryan, R. M. (1985) *Intrinsic Motivation and Self-Determination in Human Behaviour*, New York: Plenum Press.

Drust, D., Reilly, T. and Williams, A. M. (2009) *International Research in*

Science and Soccer: the proceedings of the First World Conference on Science and Soccer, London: Routledge.

Duda, J., Chi, L., Newton, M. L., Walling, M. D. and Cately, D. (1995) 'Task and ego-orientation and intrinsic motivation in sport', *International Journal of Sport Psychology*, 26: 40–63.

Fairhurst, G. T. (2008) 'Discursive leadership: a communication alternative to leadership psychology', *Management Communication Quarterly*, 21: 510–21.

Fforde, M. (2009) *Desocialisation: the crisis of post-modernity*, Cheadle Hume: Gabriel Communications.

Fischer, W. (1970) *Theories of Anxiety*, New York: Harper & Row.

Frankl, V. (1984) *Man's Search for Meaning: An Introduction to Logotherapy*, New York: Simon & Schuster.

Freud, S. (1991) *Civilization and its Discontents*, New York: W.W. Norton & Company.

Gilbourne, D. and Richardson, D. (2005) 'A practitioner focused approach to the provision of psychological support in soccer: adopting action research themes and processes', *Journal of Sports Sciences*, 23: 651–8.

—— (2006). 'Tales from the field: personal reflections on the provision of psychological support in professional soccer', *Psychology of Sport and Exercise*, 7: 335–7.

Gilmore, S. E. and Gilson, C. H. J. (2007) 'Finding form: elite sports and the business of change, *Journal of Organization Change Management*, 20: 409–23.

Gilson, C., Pratt, M., Roberts, K. and Weymes, E. (2001) *Peak Performance: business lessons from the world's top sports organizations*, London: HarperCollins.

Giorgi, A. (1970) *Psychology as a Human Science*, New York: Harper & Row.

Giorgi, A. (2000) 'Psychology as a Human science', *Journal of Humanistic Psychology*, 40: 56–73.

Glendon, M. A. (2006) *Traditions in Turmoil*, Ave Maria University: Sapientia Press.

Goldberg, A. S. (1998) *Sports Slump Busting: 10 steps to mental toughness and peak performance,* Champaign, IL: Human Kinetics.

Gould, D. (2001) *Goal Setting for Peak Performance*, Greensboro, NC: University of North Carolina.

Gould, D., Dieffenback, K. and Moffett, A. (2002) 'Psychological talent and its development in Olympic champions', *Journal of Applied Sport Psychology*, 14: 177–210.

Hardy, L. (1997) 'Three myths about applied consultancy work', *Journal of Applied Sport Psychology*, 9: 277–94.

Jackson, S. and Csikszentmihalyi, M. (1999) *Flow in Sports*, Champaign, IL: Human Kinetics.

Jones, G. (1995) 'More than just a game: research developments and issues in competitive anxiety in sport', *British Journal of Psychology*, 86: 449–78.

Jones, G., Hanton, S. and Connaughton, D. (2002) 'What is this thing called mental toughness? An investigation of elite sport performers', *Journal of Applied Sport Psychology*, 14: 205–18.

—— (2007) 'A framework of mental toughness in the world's best performers', *The Sport Psychologist*, 21: 243–64.

Kierkegaard, S. (1944 [1844]) *The Concept of Dread*, trans. S. Lowrie, Princeton, NJ: Princeton University Press (originally published in Danish).

Knowles, Z., Gilbourne, D., Tomlinson, D. and Anderson, A. (2007) 'Reflections on the application of reflective practice for supervision in applied sport psychology', *The Sport Psychologist*, 21: 109–22.

Kremer, J. and Scully, D. (2002) 'The team just hasn't gelled', in I. Cockerill (ed.), *Solutions in Sport Psychology*, London: Thomson, pp. 3–15.

Kuhn, T. (1977) *The Essential Tension: selected studies in scientific tradition and change*, Chicago, IL: University of Chicago Press.

Kuhn, T. and Jackson, M. (2008) 'Accomplishing knowledge: a framework for investigating knowing in organizations', *Management Communication Quarterly*, 21: 454–85.

Lindsay, P., Breckon, J. D., Thomas, D. and Maynard, I. (2007) 'In pursuit of congruence: a personal reflection on methods and philosophy in applied practice', *The Sport Psychologist*, 21: 335–52.

Littlewood, M. (2005). 'The impact of foreign player acquisition on the development and progression of young players in elite level English professional football', unpublished PhD thesis, Liverpool John Moores University, UK.

Magee, J. (2002) 'Shifting balances of power in the new football economy', in J. Sugden and A. Tomlinson (eds), *Power Games: a critical sociology of sport*, London: Routledge, pp. 216–39.

Marcel, G. (1948) *The Philosophy of Existence*, London: Harvill.

194

Martens, R. (1979) 'About smocks and jocks', *Journal of Sport Psychology*, 1: 94–9.

Martens, R. (1987) 'Science, knowledge, and sport psychology', *The Sport Psychologist*, 1: 29–55.

Maslow, A. H. (1968) *Toward a Psychology of Being*, New York: Van Nostrand Reinhold Company.

May, R. (1975) *The Courage to Create*, New York: Norton.

—— (1977) *The Meaning of Anxiety*, New York: Ronald Press.

—— (1995) 'Origins and significance of existential psychology', in K. J. Schneider and R. May (eds), *The Psychology of Existence: an integrative and clinical perspective,* New York: McGraw-Hill, pp. 82–8.

Maynard, I. W. and Cotton, P. C. (1993) 'An investigation of two stress-management techniques in a field setting', *The Sport Psychologist*, 7: 375–87.

Moore, Z. (2003) 'Ethical dilemmas in sport psychology: discussion and recommendations for practice', *Professional Psychology: research and practice*, 34: 601–10.

Murphy, M. and White, R. A. (1995) *In the Zone: transcendent experience in sports*, London: Penguin.

Murray, M. C. and Mann, B. L. (2001) 'Leadership effectiveness', in J. Williams (ed.), *Applied Sport Psychology: personal growth to peak performance*, Palo Alto, CA: Mayfield Publishing Company, pp. 83–106.

Nesti, M. (2002) 'Meaning not measurement: existential psychology approaches to counselling in sport contexts', in D. Lavallee and I. Cockerill (eds), *Counselling in Sport and Exercise Contexts*, Leicester: British Psychological Society, Sport and Exercise Psychology Section, pp. 38–47.

—— (2004) *Existential Psychology and Sport: theory and application,* London: Routledge.

—— (2007) 'Persons and players', in Parry, J., Nesti, M. S., Robinson, S. and Watson, N. (eds), *Sport and Spirituality: an introduction*, London: Routledge, pp. 135–50.

Nesti, M. and Sewell, D. (1999) 'Losing it: the importance of anxiety and mood stability in sport', *Journal of Personal and Interpersonal Loss*, 4: 257–68.

Nesti, M. and Littlewood, M. (2009) 'Psychological preparation and development of players in premiership football: practical and theoretical perspectives', in T. Riley, A. M. Williams and B. Drust (eds),

International Research in Science and Soccer, London: Routledge, pp. 169–76.

——— (in press) 'Making your way in the game: boundary situations within the world of professional football', in D. Gilbourne and M. Andersen (eds), *Critical Essays in Sport Psychology*, Champaign, IL: Human Kinetics.

Nicholls, A. R. (2007) 'A longitudinal phenomenological analysis of coping effectiveness among Scottish international adolescent golfers', *European Journal of Sport Science*, 7: 169–78.

——— (2008) 'Stress and coping among international adolescent golfers: applied implications, *Sport and Exercise Psychology Review*, 4: 5–9.

Orlick, T. (2000) *In Pursuit of Excellence: how to win in sport and life through mental training*, Champaign, IL: Human Kinetics.

Pain, M. and Harwood, C. (2007) 'The performance environment of the England youth soccer teams', *Journal of Sports Sciences*, 25: 1307–24.

Parker, A. (1995) 'Great expectations: grimness or glamour? The football apprentice in the 1990s', *The Sports Historian*, 15: 107–26.

——— (1996) 'Professional football culture: Goffman, asylums and occupational socialization', *Scottish Centre Research Papers in Sport, Leisure and Society*, 1: 123–30.

——— (2001) 'Soccer, servitude and sub-cultural identity: football traineeship and masculine construction', *Soccer and Society*, 2: 59–80.

Pieper, J. (1989) *Josef Pieper: an anthology*, San Francisco, CA: Ignatius Press.

——— (1995) *Divine Madness: Plato's case against secular humanism*, San Francisco, CA: Ignatius Press.

Pilgrim, D. and Treacher, A. (1992) *Clinical Psychology Observed*, London: Routledge.

Polanyi, M. (1958) *Personal Knowledge,* Chicago, IL: University of Chicago Press.

The Political Economy of Football (2008) 'English Premier League TV Broadcast Rights – 2007/2010'. Available online at: http://www.footballeconomy.com/stats/stats_tv_04.htm (accessed June 10, 2008).

Pummell, B., Harwood, C. and Lavallee, D. (2008) 'Jumping to the next level: a qualitative examination of within-career transitions in adolescent event riders', *Psychology of Sport and Exercise*, 9: 427–47.

Ravizza, K. (1977) 'Peak experiences in sport', *Journal of Humanistic Psychology*, 17: 35–40.

196

—— (2002a) 'A philosophical construct: a framework for performance enhancement', *International Journal of Sport Psychology*, 33: 4–18.

—— (2002b) 'Spirituality and peak experiences', symposia conducted at the Annual Conference of the American Association of Applied Sports Psychology, Tuscon, AZ, 30 October–3 November 2002.

Relvas, H., Littlewood, M., Nesti, M., Gilbourne, D. and Richardson, D. (2010) 'Organizational structures and working practices in elite European professional football clubs', *European Sport Management Quarterly*, 10: 165–87.

Richardson, D., Gilbourne, D. and Littlewood, M. (2004) 'Developing support mechanisms for elite young players in a professional soccer academy', *European Sport Management Quarterly*, 4: 195–214.

Robinson, S. (2007) 'Spirituality, sport and virtues', in J. Parry, M. S. Nesti, S. Robinson and N. Watson (eds), *Sport and Spirituality: an introduction*, London: Routledge, pp. 173–85.

Roderick, M. (2006) *The Work of Professional Football: a labour of love*, London: Routledge.

Rotella, R. J. (1990) 'Providing sport psychology consulting services to professional athletes', *Sport Psychologist*, 4: 409–17.

Salter, D. (1997) 'Measure, analyse and stagnate: towards a radical psychology of sport, in R. J. Butler (ed.), *Sports Psychology in Performance*, Oxford: Reed Educational and Professional Publishing, pp. 248–60.

Sartre, J. P. (1958) *Being and Nothingness*, New York: The Philosophical Library.

Silva, J., Conroy, D. E. and Zizzi, S. J. (1999) 'Critical issues confronting the advancement of applied sport psychology', *Journal of Applied Sport Psychology*, 11: 298–320.

Sparkes, A. (2002) *Telling Tales in Sport and Physical Activity: a qualitative journey*, Champaign, IL: Human Kinetics.

Thelwell, R., Weston, N. and Greenlees, I. (2005) 'Defining and understanding mental toughness within soccer', *Journal of Applied Sport Psychology*, 17: 326–32.

Van Kaam, A. (1969) *Existential Foundations of Psychology*, New York: Image.

Vitz, P. (1994) *Psychology as Religion: the cult of self-worship*, Grand Rapids, MI: Williams Eerdmans.

Watson, N. and Nesti, M. (2005) 'The role of spirituality in sport psychology consulting: an analysis and integrative review of literature', *Journal of Applied Sport Psychology*, 17: 228–334.

Williams, J. M. (ed.) (2006) *Applied Sport Psychology: personal growth to peak performance*, New York: McGraw-Hill.

Wilson, A. M. (2001) 'Understanding organisational culture and the implications for corporate marketing', *European Journal of Marketing*, 35: 353–67.

Woodman, T. and Hardy, L. (2001) 'A case study of organizational stress in elite sport', *Journal of Applied Sport Psychology*, 13: 207–38.

INDEX

204